❧ M O D E R N ❧ I R I S H ❧ W R I T E R S ❧

General Editor: W. R. Owens

W. B. Yeats

P. N. FURBANK

D1807859

❧ MODERN ❧ IRISH ❧ WRITERS ❧

General Editor: W. R. Owens

W. B. YEATS
P. N. Furbank

JAMES JOYCE
Graham Martin and Dennis Walder

❧ M O D E R N ❧ I R I S H ❧ W R I T E R S ❧

W. B. Yeats

P. N. FURBANK

THE OPEN UNIVERSITY   CENTRE FOR CONTINUING EDUCATION

The Open University Press

PA710   PACK DEVELOPMENT TEAM
W. R. Owens (chairman)
Joan Bellamy (author)
P. N. Furbank (author)
Stephanie McKnight (course co-ordinator)
Celia Wathen (editor)
Magnus John (liaison librarian)
Joanna Tregartha (designer)
John Bradley (design group co-ordinator)
Jack Clegg (audio producer)
Geoffrey Bourne (academic co-ordinator for
Personal and Cultural Education)

The Open University Press
Walton Hall, Milton Keynes
MK7 6AA

First published 1983

Designed by the Graphic Design Group of the Open University

Printed in Great Britain by
Staples Printers St Albans Limited at The Priory Press

ISBN 0 335 10435 5

For general availability of OU teaching material referred to in this text, please write to
Open University Educational Enterprises Limited, 12 Cofferidge Close, Stony
Stratford, Milton Keynes, MK11 1BY, Great Britain.
Further information on Open University continuing education courses may be obtained
from A.S.C.O., The Open University, PO Box 76, Walton Hall, Milton Keynes, MK7 6AN
1.1

Contents

Acknowledgements

Grateful acknowledgement is made to the following for permission to reproduce material in this book:

Michael B. Yeats, Anne Yeats and Macmillan, London and Basingstoke, for:

'The Indian to his Love' from *The Collected Poems of W. B. Yeats*; 'An Indian Song' from *The Variorum Edition of the Poems of W. B. Yeats*; W. B. Yeats, *A Vision*; and W. B. Yeats, *Essays and Introductions*.

Introductory Study Guide

The poet W. H. Auden once defined poetry as 'memorable speech', and there could hardly be a better way to describe the central quality of W. B. Yeats's best poetry. Proudly eloquent, musical and dramatic, it celebrates beauty, love, courage, energy, the sheer excitement of being alive in words which remain ringing in one's mind and become part of one's consciousness. The rewards offered by such poetry are rich indeed, and the aim of this pack of teaching material on Yeats is quite straightforward: it is to help you increase your understanding and enjoyment of his poetry, and equip you to go further into the study of his writings. As well as this booklet of teaching material, the pack includes an audio cassette containing readings of Yeats's poems and a performance of his one-act verse play, *Purgatory*. There are separate notes with the cassette. In addition you will need a collection of Yeats's poems. The edition referred to throughout the pack is *The Collected Poems of W. B. Yeats* published by Macmillan, and available in paperback.* There are useful notes and references at the back of the book relating to particular poems.

   This teaching material on Yeats has been adapted from that written by P. N. Furbank, Reader in Literature at the Open University, for the course team which produced the undergraduate course, A306 *Twentieth Century Poetry*.† That course covered major poets of this century from Thomas Hardy up to the present day and included British, European, American—as well as Irish—poets. Students of the course spend about four weeks studying the Yeats material, but you are naturally free to work on it entirely at your own pace, depending on the time you have available, your knowledge of Yeats himself and how accustomed you are to reading and studying poetry. After a short biographical introduction, the method employed in the teaching material is to work out from the detailed analysis of particular poems to a consideration of two of Yeats's most important complete books of poetry, *The Wind Among the Reeds* (1899) and *The Tower* (1928).

---

* *The Collected Poems of W. B. Yeats* (2nd edn) (1950), Macmillan, Basingstoke. Available in paperback 1982.
† The Open University (1976) *A306 Twentieth Century Poetry* (particularly Units 14–17), The Open University Press, Milton Keynes.

We have assumed that you will be working on the material on your own, though it could form a good basis for group work too. Please look on this not as yet another book, but as a *working guide*. It is a kind of dialogue between yourself as student and P. N. Furbank as tutor. You are being offered factual information, ideas, critical points of view and, above all, examples of ways of reading Yeats's poetry. From time to time P. N. Furbank will interrupt his commentary to ask you to answer some specific questions. These are marked in the text with a little shamrock motif. You will find as you proceed that you will be asked to take on an increasingly active role. When P. N. Furbank asks you to read a poem through, or consider some particular issue, please do just that and take some time over it. By doing the work as prescribed you will be preparing yourself to respond to the subsequent discussion more knowledgeably and more actively. Most of us learn by 'doing' and you will get much more out of this study material if you treat it as a 'work book'. We hope that as you follow through the working method offered here you will develop your own ways of close and critical reading which will enrich your pleasure in the work of Ireland's greatest poet.

If you are already used to reading and studying poetry you will probably have your own personal way of engaging with poems, and identifying your responses to them. But if you are new to it or coming back after a long interval these few points might be useful. Think of yourself as exploring a poem, as finding ways of 'moving into' it. Try to come to the poem free of pre-conceptions or prejudices, even if you do already have some knowledge of it. Be prepared to read it a number of times. You may enjoy it the very first time you read it, but almost certainly it will offer fuller and richer meanings as you get to know it better. Try reading it aloud; that will force you to decide what stress, colour and significance to give to particular words, particular images, sounds and rhythms. Listen also to the cassette where readers, including Yeats himself, offer you their 'interpretations'. Any reading aloud, yours or theirs, is a way of expressing the meaning of the poem and an interpretation of it.

When you have done this, move on to working out, in note form, your own 'prose version' of the poem, thoroughly searching through it to make sure you have understood its meaning, not just in a general way, but in its details and complexity and perhaps settling for certain ambiguities and uncertainties. Try to work out how the ideas or feelings or attitudes of the poem are first offered to us and what happens to them as the poem progresses; try to decide what mood or tone is coming through to you from the poem, what kinds of attitudes are being expressed. This kind of close scrutiny of *what* is being said, becomes, inevitably, a scrutiny of *how* the poet is using language, how the words are selected and combined to create meaning. For this reason, it is important to have some knowledge of the techniques available to the poet and the terms we use to describe them, such as 'diction', 'syntax', 'metre', 'metaphor' and so on. If you are unsure about them, use the Glossary (pp. 101–4); you will find that your attention will be directed towards such terms as you work through the teaching material and poems come up for close analysis and discussion. Do remember though, that describing poetic technique for its own sake is a pretty useless sort of exercise; what we are after is an understanding of the poem's *meaning*, and it is an awareness of how the language has been put together and how it works on us to get us to respond to that meaning, that is important.

Chronological Table:
Events in Irish history
and Yeats's life

1893   *The Celtic Twilight* published; Gladstone's second Home Rule Bill defeated in Lords; Gaelic League founded by Douglas Hyde

1899   *The Wind among the Reeds* published; *The United Irishman* founded by Arthur Griffiths

1902   *Cathleen ni Hoolihan* produced

1904   Opening of The Abbey Theatre, Dublin

1905   Sinn Fein established

1907   Riots at the Abbey Theatre over J. M. Synge's *The Playboy of the Western World*; Yeats defends Synge

1910   *The Green Helmet and Other Poems* published

1911–12   Tour in America with Abbey Players; Irish Labour Party established by James Connolly and James Larkin

1913   Irish Volunteers formed; Dublin strike and lock-out

1914   Third Home Rule Bill receives royal assent; Ulster Volunteer Force are supplied with arms; *Responsibilities* published; outbreak of World War I

1915   Develops interest in Japanese Noh plays; *At the Hawk's Well* produced in London; Yeats refuses offer of a knighthood

1916   Easter Rising in Dublin; among those executed were Padraic Pearse, Thomas MacDonagh and John MacBride (Maud Gonne's husband)

1917   *The Wild Swans at Coole* published; Yeats buys Ballylee Tower; marries Georgina Hyde-Lees

1918   The Troubles begin (Black and Tans)

1919   Lecture tour in America; first meeting of Dail Eireann

1920   *Michael Robartes and the Dancer* published

1921   Partition of Ireland; Anglo-Irish Treaty signed

1922   Civil War breaks out; Yeats becomes member of Irish Senate

1923   Yeats awarded the Nobel Prize for Literature

1924   *Meditations in Time of Civil War* published

1925   First version of *A Vision* published

1926   Fianna Fail party established by Eamonn de Valera

1928   *The Tower* published

1929   Censorship of Publications Act

1932   *The Winding Stair and Other Poems* published

1936   Edits *The Oxford Book of Modern Verse*; IRA outlawed

1937   Revised version of *A Vision* published

1938   Last public appearance at a performance of *Purgatory* in Dublin

1939   **W. B. Yeats dies, 28 January;** buried in France

1948   (September) Yeats's body returned to Ireland for reinterment in Drumcliffe churchyard, County Sligo

Yeats the Man

W. B. Yeats (1865–1939) was for most of his long career by far the most famous and admired Irish poet. His father was the painter J. B. Yeats, and his mother was daughter of a wealthy Sligo shipowner, William Pollexfen. At the time of Yeats's birth in 1865 his father was still an art student, and the family were living in London, where they remained for some years. All through their childhood, however, the poet and his brother and sister spent long periods in Ireland, at their grandparents' house, and they came to regard Sligo, where J. B. Yeats also had relatives, as their true home. Yeats recalled this feeling in his memoir *Reveries Over Childhood and Youth:*

> A poignant memory came upon me the other day while I was passing the drinking-fountain near Holland Park, for there I and my sister had spoken together of our longing for Sligo and our hatred of London. I know we were both very close to tears and remember with wonder, for I had never known any one that cared for such mementoes, that I longed for a sod of earth from some field I knew, something of Sligo to hold in my hand.
> (*Autobiographies*, p. 31)

The Irish society Yeats was born into was Protestant and Unionist, and as a boy he learned to look down somewhat upon the Catholic population, though at the same time—this was common among the Anglo-Irish—he was brought up to feel a superiority towards the English; the elder Yeats scoffed at English public school ethics, and the poet, when he read at school about famous English victories like Crécy and Agincourt, did not feel he was reading about his own people.

Yeats's father was a remarkable man, said to have been one of the greatest conversationalists of the age. Yeats idolized his father but found him overpowering and domineering; and eventually, as a young man, he felt he must shake off his influence. He succeeded so effectively that in later years it was as though he were the father and J. B. Yeats the admiring and irresponsible son. Many of his deepest beliefs and attitudes, however, derived from his father. It was from his father that he learned his admiration for all that was vigorous,

6

reckless, passionate and unselfseeking. And conversely it was, no doubt, because his father was a Victorian rationalist (an acquaintance described him as 'singularly uncurious about God and immortality') that Yeats, very early, took a bent in the opposite direction—towards mythology, fairy-lore and the occult.

The Yeats family returned to Ireland in 1880, taking up residence in the environs of Dublin. At his new school Yeats, in the words of Joseph Hone, 'stood ostentatiously aloof from the generality of the boys. He wrapped himself in a dream of superiority, as an artist and the son of an artist, and made no attempt to conquer prejudice'. His happiest times were his holidays with his Uncle George Pollexfen in Sligo, and at this period he dreamed of living a solitary life upon the little island of Innisfree in Lough Gill. At the age of seventeen he wrote a long poem on a thicket, and, as he said long afterwards, this thicket gave him his first notion of what a long poem should be: 'a region into which one might wander from the cares of life', with characters 'no more real than the shadows that people the thicket'.

From school he proceeded to the Metropolitan School of Art in Dublin, where he studied painting, with no great success. Through the acquaintance of the old Fenian leader John O'Leary, however, he was drawn into nationalist political circles; and at much the same time, under the influence of a young Indian Brahmin, Mohini Chatterji, he became interested in the occult and, with one or two friends, founded a Hermetic Society. He had also begun to publish poems in Dublin literary periodicals.

In 1887 the Yeatses returned to London again. By now Yeats, partly through O'Leary's influence, had begun to receive commissions from publishers for compilations from Irish myth and literature; and in 1889 he published his first book of verse, *The Wanderings of Oisin and Other Poems*. It won him a reputation, and on the strength of it he rapidly found his way into literary and intellectual life in London. He was drawn into the Socialist circle of William Morris, who lived near the Yeatses in Hammersmith, and likewise into the literary circle of the poet Henley. He also joined the Theosophical Society of Madame Blavatsky. It was a revealing episode: Yeats grew impatient with the high-minded vagueness of the discussions and determined to undertake some actual experiments in the occult. He had read in some seventeenth-century book that if you burned a flower to ashes and put the ashes under the receiver of an air-pump, and if then you stood the receiver in the moonlight for so many nights, the ghost of the flower would appear hovering over the ashes. He got together a committee to conduct this experiment, which proved unsuccessful; and shortly afterwards the Secretary asked him politely to resign, as he was upsetting the other members.

In 1890 he was initiated into the English branch of the recently formed Order of the Golden Dawn, a mystical fraternity based on the teachings of Rosicrucianism and the Jewish Cabbala. Here his energies were more appreciated, and before long he came to dominate the society. He was much addicted, then and later, to telepathic experiments and believed he could control his friends' thoughts by meditating upon appropriate symbols. He also found material for poetry by a mystical technique of 'putting the will to sleep' and allowing symbols to rise and proliferate before the mind's eye.

At about the same time, with two friends, he founded the Rhymers' Club, a group which became famous and included many of the leading poets of the 1890s such as Lionel Johnson, John Davidson, Ernest Dowson, Richard le Gallienne and Arthur Symons. This does not end the list of Yeats's activities at this time. In 1891, for instance, he founded an Irish Literary Society in London, the parent of a chain of such societies in Ireland itself.

Socialism soon lost his support; but his other three interests, poetry, the occult and the creation, through literature, of a revived sense of national identity for Ireland, remaining the ruling ones of his life. They were, you might say, different aspects of the same interest. Thus, he saw it as the ambition of poetry to revive the deeper imaginative life, starved by modern urban existence, and he could picture this as achieved equally through ancient Celtic legend and myth, or through occult sciences like 'spiritualism', Rosicrucianism or Swedenborgianism. Similarly, the goal or ideal he pictured for Ireland was what he called 'Unity of Culture', a spiritual unity overriding class and religious differences; and this was close to his ideal in personal life, which was a 'Unity of Being', a harmony in which the soul did not prey on the body and the life of feeling was not poisoned by overdevotion to 'abstract' causes.

His reputation as a poet grew quickly, and during the early 1890s he became very influential as the leader of a literary movement which became known as the 'Celtic Twilight'. The name (rudely parodied later by James Joyce as 'the cultic toilette') was invented by Yeats himself, who in 1893 published a volume of tales called *The Celtic Twilight*. The movement owed much to the French Symbolist poets of the preceding two decades and represented a revolt against the positivistic and materialistic tendencies of nineteenth-century life and of mid-nineteenth century theories of art and literature. It rejected the notion that art and literature should serve social good and deal with human problems in a 'scientific' and rationalist manner, and its poetry struck a note of ethereality, world-weariness and quietism. This note was in fact deceptive, for what underlay the movement was a vigorous political purpose, no less than the regeneration of the Irish race.

Two events of great importance in his personal life happened at this period. In January 1889 he met Maud Gonne (1866–1953), another of O'Leary's protégées. She was the daughter of a Dublin Castle official

W. B. Yeats by J. B. Yeats (1900). (National Gallery of Ireland)

John O'Leary (the Fenian leader) by J. B. Yeats. (National Gallery of Ireland)

but had abandoned Castle society and fashionable life for extremist nationalist politics. She was tall, magnificently beautiful and a brilliant and emotional platform orator, and Yeats and she recognised each other as predestined allies. He also fell profoundly in love with her—a frustrating love affair which obsessed and dominated him for twenty years. Through her he was drawn further into nationalist politics, even becoming for a short time a member of the Irish Republican Brotherhood, the 'physical force' wing of the nationalists. At one one time he and Maud Gonne planned, half-seriously, a Castle of Heroes, a shrine in the middle of a lake to which only those might penetrate who had dedicated their lives to Ireland.

The second major event was that in 1896, while staying with a friend in Galway, he met Lady Augusta Gregory (1852–1932), a wealthy middle-aged widow, owner of a fine estate at Coole Park. She appointed herself his patron and encouraged him to regard Coole Park, with its lake and seven woods, as a second home; and through his influence she took to writing herself and became his associate in the Irish literary movement. With the aid of Lady Gregory, the novelist George Moore and another Irish friend and writer Edward Martyn, Yeats, in 1898, launched the Irish Literary Theatre. The original scheme was to stage, each spring in Dublin, Celtic and Irish plays which—so the prospectus announced—would aim at expressing 'the deeper thoughts and emotions of Ireland'. Then, in 1903, Miss Horniman, a wealthy friend of his in the Order of the Golden Dawn, offered him a theatre of his own in Dublin, the one which was to become famous as the Abbey Theatre.

For the next ten years or so his Irish theatre became the centre of Yeats's activities. He wrote numerous plays for it himself, but perhaps the greatest achievement of the movement was his discovery of the playwright J. M. Synge. Synge's plays on Irish themes realised to the full Yeat's ambition for 'a national literature that made Ireland beautiful in the memory, and yet had been freed from provincialism by an exacting criticism, a European pose'. The plays, however, ruffled local susceptibilities, and Synge's *The Playboy of the Western World*, in some ways very satirical of the Irish, caused riots on its first performance in 1907. For Yeats, who believed the hostility hastened Synge's early death, this was a never-to-be-forgotten night, epitomizing the division between a chauvinistic nationalism and the deeper and visionary kind that he and his friends believed in.

After Synge's death in 1909—and, ironically, partly as a result of his influence—the Abbey Theatre took a turn towards realism and character-comedy which displeased Yeats, who believed in a drama that should be remote, ideal and spiritual, and he gradually withdrew from its activities. He still had strong ambitions as a playwright, and, having been introduced by the American poet Ezra Pound to the Japanese *Noh* plays, he attempted something equivalent—verse plays

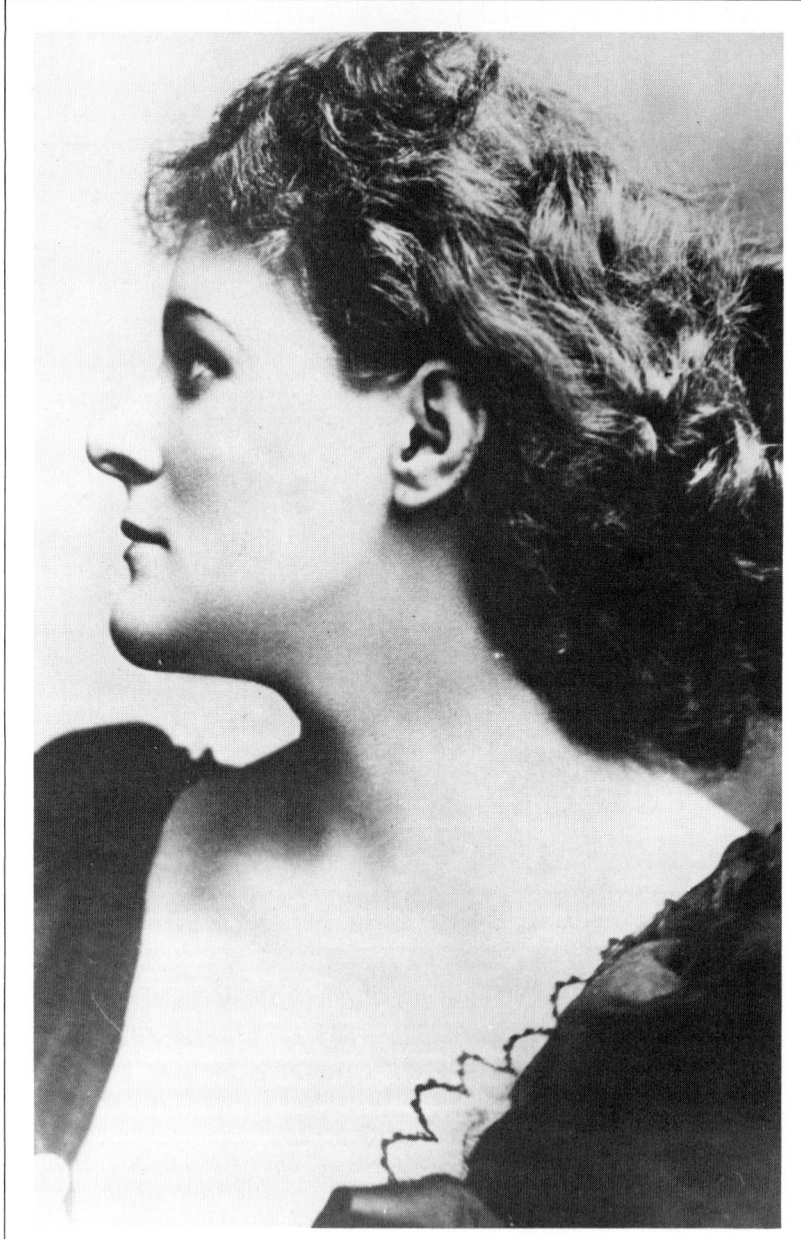

Maude Gonne. (National Museum of Ireland)

on Celtic themes, rigidly stylized and formal in their action and staging, with their meaning coming to a focus in songs.

During his theatrical period Yeats wrote relatively little lyric verse and felt to some extent that he had lost his direction as a lyric poet. The early twentieth century was rather a low ebb in verse generally, and Yeats tended to feel himself a lonely survivor of the ill-fated school of the 1890s. Somewhere about 1910 or 1912, however—and perhaps to some extent through the influence of Ezra Pound, whom Yeats got to know at this time—Yeats moved towards a new stage in his career as a lyric poet. He describes the change in a letter to his father of July 1913:

> . . . of recent years instead of vision, meaning by vision the intense realisation of ecstatic emotion symbolised in a definite imagined region, I have tried for more self-portraiture, I have tried to make my work convincing with a speech so natural that the hearer would feel the presence of a man thinking and feeling. There are always the two types of poetry—Keats, the type of vision, Burns a very obvious type of the other, too obvious indeed. It is in dramatic lyrical expression that English poetry is most lacking as compared with French poetry. Villon always and Ronsard at times create marvellous drama out of their own lives.

He had found a way beyond his 'Celtic twilight' manner, that cultivation of tenuousness and shadowiness, and in forging a new style he found he was helped by his theatrical experience. He said later, in *Dramatis Personae* (1936):

> In dream poetry, in *Kubla Khan*, in *The Stream's Secret* [a poem by Swinburne] every line, every word, can carry its unanalysable, rich associations; but if we dramatize some possible singer or speaker we remember that he is moved by one thing at a time, certain words must be dull and numb. Here and there in correcting my early poems I have introduced such numbers and dullness, turning, for instance, 'the curd-pale moon' [in the poem 'The Sorrow of Love'] into the 'brilliant moon', that all might seem, as it were, remembered with indifference except for some one vivid image.
> (*Autobiographies*, pp. 434–435)

The coming of war did not affect Yeats deeply in any personal sense. He felt, as did many of the Irish, that it was not *his* war, an attitude which finds expression in his fine poem 'An Irish Airman Foresees His Death' ('Those that I fight I do not hate/Those that I guard I do not love . . .'). The event which succeeded in stirring him was the Easter Rising of 1916. He was staying with friends in Gloucestershire at the time and had grown somewhat out of touch with developments in his own country, so the rebellion took him as much by surprise as it did his English friends. Most of the leaders executed for their part in the Rising were acquaintances of his; and to complicate his feelings, one of these men was his hated rival Major John MacBride, who had married, and cruelly misused, Maud Gonne twelve years before. His first reaction was, in fact, a certain pique that he had not been consulted before the Rising, but other emotions supervened, and in a month or two he had composed his moving elegy 'Easter 1916' (*Collected Poems*, pp. 202–205) treating these events not as a mere rebellion but as a revolution.

The death of MacBride left Maud Gonne a free woman, and Yeats once more proposed marriage. Refused, he proposed to her beautiful daughter Iseult,* and on being rejected by her likewise, he acknowledged an end to that dream, and in 1917 married Georgina Hyde-Lees, a friend of some years' standing. The marriage was a most successful one; and it had an unexpected bonus for Yeats in that his wife turned out to have mediumistic powers and, four days after their wedding, volunteered to attempt automatic writing. The messages Yeats received through her from mysterious 'communicators' so excited him that he offered to spend the rest of his life studying their scattered sentences. To this offer he received the answer: 'No, we have come to give you metaphors for poetry.' He ignored the admonition, and in the years to come constructed an elaborate metaphysical system on the basis of their messages. This was published as *A Vision* in 1925, and in a drastically revised version in 1937, but, to Yeats's chagrin, was received by his admirers mainly with stony silence (see Appendix II).

He was by the 1920s a much-fêted public figure, and in 1923 he was awarded the Nobel prize. In the previous year, at the height of the Civil War in Ireland, he had been appointed by the Irish Free State Government as a member of their first Senate. For Maud Gonne, who was deeply involved on the Republican side (i.e., those who refused to recognise the partition of Ireland established by the treaty with Britain of December 1921) his acceptance was a betrayal and meant that politically he was past redemption. He did indeed in later years become more outspokenly anti-democratic in his politics, and for a brief period in the 1930s he became involved with the semi-fascist 'Blueshirt' movement of General O'Duffy.

The four collections of verse which followed the 1914–18 war, *The Wild Swans at Coole* (1919), *Michael Robartes and the Dancer* (1921), *The Tower* (1928), and *The Winding Stair and Other Poems* (1933) revealed unmistakably the new directions he had taken as a poet. Lyric poetry was once more his central concern; and, being now himself an ageing man, he found in the theme of old age, which had haunted him from his earliest youth, the material for some of his most

*Iseult was her illegitimate daughter by a French journalist called Millevoye.

powerful verse. His contemporaries sometimes regretted the disappearance of the earlier Yeats, the exquisite Romantic singer and dreamer, but most critics would now agree that the later Yeats—the Yeats, at least, of the 1920s—was the greater one.

As for Yeats the man, as he was at this later period, people form different judgements. The Yeats of *The Tower*, and even more the Yeats of some of the songs in *Last Poems*, can appear a rancorous and desperate man. Those who take this view of him are offended by his epigram 'The Spur' (*Collected Poems*, p. 359):

> You think it horrible that lust and rage
> Should dance attention upon my old age;
> They were not such a plague when I was young;
> What else have I to spur me into song?

T. S. Eliot, however, makes a persuasive defence of the lines. He says:

> These lines are very impressive and not very pleasant and the senti-
> ment has recently been criticised by an English critic whom I
> generally respect [presumably F. R. Leavis]. But I think he has mis-
> read them. I do not read them as a personal confession of a man who
> differed from other men, but of a man who was essentially the same
> as most other men; the only difference is in the greater clarity,
> honesty and vigour. To what honest man, old enough, can these
> sentiments be entirely alien?
> (Eliot, *On Poets and Poetry*, 1957, pp. 257–258)

It seems plain, at least, that the ageing Yeats felt, at times, an exultant sense of having triumphed over age and decay. In a dedication to *The Winding Stair*, addressed to Edmund Dulac, he has these impressive words:

> 'A Dialogue of Self and Soul' was written in the spring of 1928 during
> a long illness, indeed finished the day before a Cannes doctor told me
> to stop writing. Then in the spring of 1929 life returned as an impres-
> sion of the uncontrollable energy and daring of the great creators: it
> seemed that but for journalism and criticism, all that evasion and
> explanation, the world would be torn to pieces.
> (*Collected Poems*, pp. 536–537)

The question of Yeats's character is a large and fascinating subject. Anyone who has looked at his prose writings, his essays and *Autobiographies*, has to recognise him as a most formidable man: not only superbly intelligent but extremely witty and a profound judge of men. He was also arrogant, wilful and capable of much self-delusion; but he was not, I would say, an egotistical man. In 1930 he made this odd and interesting remark in his diary: '. . . my character is so little myself that all my life it has thwarted me. It has affected my poems,

my true Self, no more than the character of a dancer affects the movement of a dance'. One characteristic he had which affects all the rest:
he regarded life as a drama, a stage play, played out before a real or
imaginary audience. One feels that he is a man on stilts, and one
sometimes wishes that he would get down off them. He knew this trait
of his own very clearly and said that he acquired it, or was encouraged
in it, at the Rhymers' Club, where a certain formal stiffness and pose
was the rule. Maybe, too, it is a characteristic of Irish public men to
adopt a posture and deliberately foster a legend round themselves.
But the matter goes deeper than this. Yeats's behaviour in this respect
is part and parcel of a long-pondered theory of life and is the logical
consequence of his theory of the mask.

Masks and Anti-selves

Yeats conceived of all human life, but especially the life of artists, as proceeding by contraries. The creative man sets himself in motion by attempting to create, or realise, an imaginary self, an 'anti-self', which is the very opposite of all that he is in daily life. Thus, to take his own examples, the solitary and physically frail Synge, who wrote riotous and life-affirming comedies, was 'a sick man picturing energy, a doomed man picturing gaiety'. Or, again, William Morris, an extremely energetic and irascible man who once threw a badly cooked Christmas pudding through the window, wrote, as a poet, of faint, melancholy, medieval figures 'who are never, no, not once in fifty volumes, put out of temper' (*Autobiographies*, p. 143). The same would be true of Yeats himself:

> I know very little about myself and much less about that anti-self: probably the woman who cooks my dinner or the woman who sweeps out my study knows more than I. It is perhaps because Nature made me a gregarious man, going hither and thither looking for conversation, and ready to deny from fear or favour his dearest conviction, that I love proud and lonely things.
> (*Autobiographies*, p. 171)

In Yeats's view there is nothing here to invalidate the work of such writers. A writer's or artist's life is in its very nature a conflict and a battle between opposed contraries. And for this reason a writer's life is, of necessity, tragic. 'We begin to live when we have conceived life as tragedy', he says. On the other hand—and here lies its compensation—a writer's life is a daily triumph over age and decay. 'Among subjective men (in all those, that is, who must spin a web out of their own bowels) the victory is an intellectual daily re-creation of all that exterior fate snatches away, and so that fate's antithesis...' (*Autobiographies*, p. 189).

In the poem 'Ego Dominus Tuus' ('I thy Lord'), in *The Wild Swans at Coole* (1919), Yeats makes an explicit statement of this conception of the anti-self. (You might like to look the poem up.) The poem takes the form of a dialogue between two opposed spokesmen, *Hic* (this person) and *Ille* (that person), who no doubt represent two halves of Yeats himself. *Ille* expounds the doctrine of the anti-self:

17

> By the help of an image
> I call to my own opposite, summon all
> That I have handled least, least looked upon.

But *Hic* enquires, are there not artists who produce art without all this self-conflict: 'Impulsive men that look for happiness/And sing when they have found it'? *Ille* answers 'No'. Men who are on good terms with the world serve it by action not by art, and if they do practise art, it turns out to be bad art: rhetoric or sentimentality. For to produce true art you have to renounce the world:

> What portion in the world can the artist have
> Who has awakened from the common dream
> But dissipation and despair?

There is a further thought connected with this Yeatsian doctrine of contraries, which is that virtue may arise from the recognition of evil. Thus, to take an example, the interests of Irish nationalism would be best served by satire on the Irish by Irishmen. If the Irish could only fully recognise their own weaknesses, their bragging and loquacity etc. (so Yeats thought), they might not merely improve themselves but produce the exactly opposite qualities: 'unyielding personality, manner at once cold and passionate, daring long-premeditated act'. Likewise the Irish, the most bitter of nations, might, if they could achieve self-knowledge, find a greater sweetness than has been known to any other nation. In this dynamic theory of contraries Yeats found support in his beloved hero William Blake, who said, in *The Marriage of Heaven and Hell*, 'Without contraries is no progression. Attraction and Repulsion, Reason and Energy, Love and Hate, are necessary to Human existence.' Yeats wrote, in *A Vision* (1937):

> . . . my mind had been full of Blake from boyhood up and I saw the world as a conflict . . . and could distinguish between a contrary and a negation. 'Contraries are positive', wrote Blake, 'a negation is not a contrary . . . There is a place at the bottom of graves where contraries are equally true'.

Yeats refined on these ideas of his endlessly; but even from my bald account, I think you will see that they are very rich and suggestive ideas, ones which in a way come home to most people's experience. What we can also see, though, is something particularly characteristic of Yeats himself: I mean, a strenuousness and deliberateness in his approach to life and art. He said himself, in *The Trembling of the Veil*, 'only the greatest obstacle that can be contemplated without despair raises the will to full intensity' (*Autobiographies*, p. 195). He needed the stimulus of the nearly impossible. His ambition to create a unified consciousness for the Irish race may seem overweening, but he needed an ambition on that scale. Similarly, though unquestionably he was deeply in love with Maud Gonne, one feels that he *needed* such an almost-impossible love. Again, you might say, he deliberately invented metaphysical beliefs for himself and then went ahead and believed them. Though if this is true, he was not alone in it: other poets of the early twentieth century, for instance Rilke, felt, as Yeats did, both the need to believe in some transcendent order, and the impossibility of accepting the traditional Christian version of that order, so, by means of their art, they deliberately set about creating their own objects of belief. Eliot—though he eventually found his way into the Christian church—catches precisely this 'process of thought, and its circularity', in some lines in 'Ash Wednesday':

> Consequently I rejoice, having to construct something
> Upon which to rejoice

One could almost regard this as the motto of the major poets of the early part of the century. There was much talk of a 'poetry divorced from all forms of belief' but in fact the poetry of Yeats, Eliot and Rilke was very much concerned with belief. They 'believed in belief', for all that they had to construct their beliefs through art. I would add that this likeness between Yeats and Eliot seems to me more important than superficial differences between them. One feels—or at least I feel—a deep affinity between them in their idea of what poetry can do.*

---

* It shows a decline from this confident 'modernist' attitude to art that W. H. Auden, after his conversion to Christianity, renounced all such high claims for poetry and art. He insisted that they should be regarded as no more than a marvellous game.

19

What Kind of Poet is Yeats?

My answer to this question is a simple one, yet worth giving, I think. It is that, though he lived on into a period when very bold innovations and experiments were being made in verse, and though he was greatly esteemed by those innovatory and 'modernist' writers, Yeats is a traditional poet. To be more precise, he belonged to the tradition of English Romantic poetry. He was, for one thing, content to use the traditional metres of English verse, and felt at home with them—though on the other hand, within these metres he was a great explorer and innovator, perhaps one of the greatest there has been, and he impressed an absolutely personal accent upon these rhythms. The more one reads Yeats and the better one's ear becomes attuned to him, the richer the subtleties of rhythm one finds in him.

Again, he had a 'style', whereas 'modernist' poets like T. S. Eliot and Ezra Pound tended to invent a new style for each new poem or group of poems. I do not mean that Yeats's poems are all in the same style, which of course would be absurd. He had various different styles for different purposes: noble or bawdy, lyrical or conversational, luxuriant or plain, according to his need; and later poems of his often depend upon the contrast of these various manners and tones of voice within the one poem. What I mean, rather, is that, like Milton, if he makes some successful invention in style, one can be sure he will use it again and again, continually refining upon it but never abandoning it; it will become a permanent part of his poetic equipment. His development was very much the development of a 'style', and I do not only mean a verse style; it was also the elaboration of a style, a pose, _vis-à vis_ his fellow-men, the constructing of a public role. Here again he was traditional, for poets like Milton and Virgil also composed for themselves a public and artificial poetic personality.

He was traditional, once more, in his conception of the poet's vocation. He believed that a poet was a dreamer, a man who, by licensed and controlled dreaming, could give shape to an alternative reality. This was the belief not only of Shelley and Keats, but of Milton, or of Sir Philip Sidney in his _Apology for Poetry_:

> Nature never sets forth the earth in so rich tapestry as divers poets have done—neither with pleasant rivers, fruitful trees, sweet-

smelling flowers, nor whatsoever else may make the too much loved earth more lovely.

Of course these were all men who were also passionately interested in the actual world they lived in, otherwise they could hardly have been good poets; but they felt it was part of their duty to set up an ideal 'reality' by which the common reality could be criticized. It is not the only possible view of poetry; Wordsworth did not subscribe to it, nor did Thomas Hardy.

Making an Anthology of Yeats

I propose now to select and discuss a few poems to illustrate the variety of the *kinds* of poem that Yeats wrote. They are all poems that I admire greatly, and thus you could say I am assembling my own anthology of Yeats.

Here, to begin with, is 'The Indian to his Love'. As an exercise, you might find it useful to write out short notes answering the following questions: What is the tone or mood of this poem? What do you feel about it, and why? Are there any features of the language that strike you as significant or special, and if so what do you think is their function?

You may find it a help to read the poem aloud a number of times.

The Indian to his Love

The island dreams under the dawn
And great boughs drop tranquillity;
The peahens dance on a smooth lawn,
A parrot sways upon a tree,
Raging at his own image in the enamelled sea.

Here we will moor our lonely ship
And wander ever with woven hands,
Murmuring softly lip to lip
Along the grass, along the sands,
Murmuring how far away are the unquiet lands:

How we alone of mortals are
Hid under quiet boughs apart,
While our love grows an Indian star,
A meteor of the burning heart,
One with the tide that gleams, the wings that gleam and dart,

The heavy boughs, the burnished dove
That moans and sighs a hundred days:
How when we die our shades will rove,
When eve has hushed the feathered ways,
With vapoury footsole by the water's drowsy blaze.

It is, I think you will agree, a marvellously beautiful poem, achieving in that last line an extraordinary synthesis of conflicting impressions: tenuousness and fervency, shadowiness and definition. The kind of living it celebrates, however, is the most twilit, ethereal affair imaginable, altogether a kind of death-in-life: far away indeed are ethics or effort or any active concerns. You may say that it is just 'escapist' poetry, a weak kind of dreaming such as has earned Victorian poetry a bad name; but I think you would be wrong. For is there not a vigour and challenge in its very renunciation of the busy striving world? The energies of the world have been stilled but not extinguished; indeed the poem is full of these energies—the parrot 'rages', the Indian's love, though twilit, is to burn like a meteor. What we have in this poem, I suggest, is not escapism at all, but an impassioned ascetic contemplativeness, not very different from what Yeats will express much later in his 'Byzantium' poems. There is a difference, however. The poem is very hushed and rapt, quite unlike the robustness and ribaldry of the later Yeats.

What we have in the young Yeats is something very characteristic of the period: the spectacle of very vigorous, combative, rather worldly men writing deliberately limp and 'unworldly' poems. I have cheated a little over 'The Indian to his Love', for what I have given is Yeats's final version of the poem. It is important to remember that Yeats continued revising his poems throughout his career, sometimes quite drastically. The first version, written some thirty years earlier, runs as follows:

An Indian Song

Oh wanderer in the southern weather,
    Our isle awaits us; on each lea
The pea-hens dance, in crimson feather
    A parrot swaying on a tree
    Rages at his own image in the enamelled sea.

There dreamy Time lets fall his sickle
    And Life the sandals of her fleetness,
And sleek young Joy is no more fickle,
    And Love is kindly and deceitless,
    And life is over save the murmur and the sweetness

There we will moor our lonely ship
    And wander ever with woven hands,
Murmuring softly, lip to lip,
    Along the grass, along the sands –
    Murmuring how far away are all earth's feverish lands:

> How we alone of mortals are
>   Hid in the earth's most hidden part,
> While grows our love an Indian star,
>   A meteor of the burning heart,
>   One with the waves that softly round us laugh and dart,
>
> Like swarming bees; one with the dove
>   That moans and sighs a hundred days;
> – How when we die our shades will rove,
>   Dropping at eve in coral bays,
>   A vapoury footfall on the ocean's sleepy blaze.

I hope you will agree that the later version is strikingly superior, and you might like to ponder the differences and why they might be thought to be improvements. It is a comparison that reveals a good deal about Yeats's development, and something about the development of English poetry in general in the twentieth century. The later Yeats would have been careful to avoid such slack and rather old-fashioned sounding personifications as 'dreamy Time', 'sleek young Joy' etc.

Next, please look at the song, published in 1910, called 'Brown Penny' (*Collected Poems*, p. 109). Yeats wrote such 'tuney' and ballad-like poems throughout his career, and the song 'Down by the Salley Gardens' is very akin to 'Brown Penny', though written twenty years earlier. Please look that poem up also. (*Collected Poems*, p. 22).

❧   What is the difference between them?

Discussion
'Down by the Salley Gardens' is, apparently, about love being easy, if only the lover would realise the fact. 'Brown Penny' is about love being difficult and complicated, so that one cannot begin grappling with it too soon: it demands a lifetime of study. ❧

❧   What is the tone of that last line, 'One cannot begin it too soon', though?

Discussion
If the poem has any subtlety, and I think it has, it perhaps lies in that last line: 'One cannot begin it too soon'. And I read the line as rueful. It *seems* to be saying, cheerfully, what 'Down by the Salley Gardens' says: go on and love, let nothing stop you. But actually it is saying the opposite: love is such an appallingly complicated and ghastly business

that if you are going to go in for it, you had better—poor devil—start now. I would not be surprised if Yeats had 'Down by the Salley Gardens' in mind when he wrote the later poem; and to my mind the difference between the two reveals Yeats's advance in sophistication and subtlety. 'Down by the Salley Gardens' was one of Yeats's early popular successes, and it is a charming poem, but I have always felt as an objection to it that 'weirs' is a rather far-fetched rhyme to 'tears'. The technique of 'Brown Penny' strikes me as much more accomplished; there is brilliant and hair's-breadth calculation in the way the poem, which is built up out of repetitions, culminates in the double repetition 'Ah penny, brown penny, brown penny'. What is also to be observed is that 'Brown Penny' is the last poem in the collection it belongs to, a gay and irresponsible poem ending a collection called *The Green Helmet and Other Poems*. This illustrates an important fact, that the way one poem sits beside another in a volume by Yeats can be of great significance. The structure of his volumes is very carefully designed, and in the case of certain later collections, *The Tower* (1928) and *The Winding Stair* (1933), the volume could almost be said to constitute a single long poem. ❧

Will you now look at 'The Man Who Dreamed of Faeryland' (*Collected Poems*, p. 49).

This was one of the first poems of Yeats's to catch the public fancy. (When it was published in the *National Observer* in 1891, the poet Henley, who edited the paper, went round saying: 'See what a fine thing has been written by one of my lads.') I think it is not hard to see why it made a hit. It is an intriguing poem, full of the richest Romantic suggestiveness* At a first reading or two one is left in a pleasant state of mystification, not being quite sure, for instance, what those deliciously eerie little fish and muddy-mouthed lugworms are whispering to the hero—not quite sure, and not really so much wanting to be sure; for, as often with Tennyson, one knows there is a literal meaning but feels in no hurry to arrive at it, for it may turn out less interesting than the magical 'penumbra'. Then, what a captivating opening:

> He stood among a crowd at Dromahair;†
> His heart hung all upon a silken dress

This is pure lyricism, free and spontaneous: all that one thinks of

---

* The version in *Collected Poems* is substantially revised.
† Dromahair is in Co. Leitrim, and Lissadell, Scanavin and Lugnagall are in Co. Sligo.

when one refers to poetry as 'song'. And again, how much evocative force the author can concentrate in an epithet: 'a plashy place' conjures up just the right oozy, primordial habitat for the owners of those jeering, wheedling voices. This is traditional symbolism—beasts and plants in folk myths and ballads often speak in this animistic way—but Yeats has given it his own personal colouring. That 'spired' in stanza 4, too: it is like a word that we know at the back of our minds (rather as these voices seem to come from the back or the bottom of the mind), but one will not find it (I mean this use of it) in the dictionary. It is a mixture of 'spiral', and 'spire' in the same sense as in 'church spire' (i.e., something long and upwards-pointing), and perhaps 'to spire' in its obsolete sense of 'to sprout'.

✿ Nevertheless one need not have been afraid that the prose meaning would prove disappointing. It is not so at all, I think. Let us try to sort it out. For a start, what is the connection between the respective admonitions of the fish, the lug-worm, the knot-grass and the graveyard worms? I will follow this with another question, which may help in answering the first: do not the lines about the 'woven world-forgotten isle', the 'ravelled seas' and the exultant dancers 'by the dreamless wave' strike a reminiscent chord?

Discussion
They call to mind the preceding poem, 'Who Goes With Fergus?' so much that they must be a direct reference back to it. Will you have a look at 'Who Goes with Fergus?'? In that poem too we hear of 'the deep wood's woven shade' and dancers on the shore. We are also reminded of 'The Indian to his Love' (see p. 22), which likewise evokes an eternity of tranquility on a world-forgotten isle. What this brings home to us is that what the fish, the lug-worm, the knot-grass and the graveyard worms are speaking of is one and the same: it is that same isle, which is faeryland. ✿

✿ And why should dreams of that isle be a foe to the comfort of the hero of the poem? For instance in stanza 1?

Discussion
Because, here, they suggest to the lover that there might be a place where love never changes or ends: they thus introduce a note of discontentment into his new-found happiness. ✿

✿ And in stanza 2?

Discussion

Yeats's language is much more obscure here, but I would tentatively interpret the last three lines as saying that, by not desiring or hungering after things (as the hero is now hungering after wealth and possessions), the dancers on the shore find all possible desires realised. It is perhaps a mistake to try and paraphrase that line 'It seemed the sun and moon were in the fruit': but, if we imagine the isle hung with golden tropical fruit, the sense is perhaps something to the effect that, on that isle, effort and action and taking trouble for the future are abolished: beginning and end—the Sun and Moon which nourish the fruit, and the fruit which they nourish—are one and the same. ❧

❧ And stanza 3?

Discussion

Here the island, by offering the prospect of peace, takes away the hero's relish in his own anger. ❧

❧ Stanza 4?

Discussion

Again an obscure stanza, especially in those two lines:

> Why should those lovers that no lovers miss
> Dream, until God burn Nature with a kiss?

But I think the meaning must be: 'Why should those lovers who live in a place where there is no jealousy or mourning (i.e., they are not "missed" by anyone) have to dream at all? These happy lovers and dancers are not free merely from heartbreak or money-getting or anger: they are—an even greater blessing—free from the necessity of dreaming. They will dance on oblivious till the day of judgement, the final conflagration; whereas the hero of the poem, even in his grave, tosses and turns with restless dreams'. ❧

The poem thus says something rather profound, though it says it in a playful and perhaps over-obscure manner. Its theme is in fact one which dominates much of early Yeats: the dilemma of the poet who cannot help dreaming of an ideal world and by doing so may be destroying his happiness and life in the real world. We shall find Yeats returning many times to this theme in *The Wind Among The Reeds*.

As you will have gathered, what I am doing in this section is to build up a small anthology of Yeats's poems, assembled on no particular principle save that they should be good ones. This is one way in which any lyric poet can be approached. The function of such a poet, or one of his functions, is that he should provide you with poems that are complete in themselves—poems which you can memorize and call upon for encouragement, or relief, or as the perfect expression of a particular state of feeling. This may sound an old-fashioned conception of poetry, however I stand by it; and at all events it was the tradition that Yeats was bred in. In his early days particularly, he was a prolific producer of 'anthology poems'. The most famous was 'The Lake Isle of Innisfree', which he chanted in a hundred lecture halls and drawing-rooms. It was a somewhat uncharacteristic poem, more unabashedly sentimental than was usual with him, and it rather hung round his neck, so that he grew sick of it. Nevertheless, it was one of his ambitions to be a popular poet: to write poems that would find their way among people who might not even care to know who they were by. He liked to fancy himself as one of the wandering Irish bards, like the blind poet Raftery—still a living memory in his youth. C. K. Stead (1964), has written very well of Yeats's double attitude in this matter: his wish to write for 'the people', not just for a few fellow poets, but on the other hand his feeling that what readers in his day had learned to demand from verse—opinions, anecdotes, 'improving' ideas, and so on—was totally alien to true poetry. His whole career can, from one point of view, be seen as an effort to resolve this problem.

When one comes to a poem like 'The Cold Heaven' (first published in 1912) one no longer thinks of Irish bards; nor is it what one would normally call an 'anthology poem'. A poem such as this makes us very curious about the man who wrote it, as one is curious about the author of *King Lear*; as Eliot said in his 'Yeats' lecture,* it 'makes one sit up in excitement and eagerness to learn more about the author's mind and feelings'. Nevertheless there is a sense, a very honourable sense, in which this too is an 'anthology poem'; I mean, we do not *have* to know anything about the man Yeats, or his beliefs, in order to enjoy it. The poem is sufficient in itself; it records an experience so accurately and memorably that it becomes a permanent addition to the possible ways of human feeling. I do not mean that it does not refer to beliefs and ideas outside itself; for of course the poem, and especially its last lines, alludes to the Catholic doctrine of Purgatory. The poet, prompted by the spectacle of a cold winter sky, relives a past love affair with blinding clarity and blames himself so passionately for its failure that his pangs—so he thinks the next moment—must be like those of a dead man's soul beginning its purgation. However, what particular 'books' they are that speak of the ghosts of the newly dead as wandering the roads ('sent/Out naked on the

---

* Delivered to the Friends of the Irish Academy at the Abbey Theatre in 1940. Reprinted in *On Poetry and Poets*.

roads, as the books say,') is not important; nor is it important, though of course it is interesting, to know whether Yeats's idea of Purgatory is orthodox. (Eliot thought it was not; he said of Yeats's late play *Purgatory* (1938) 'I wish he had not given it this title, because I cannot accept a purgatory in which there is no hint, or at least no emphasis upon Purgation'.) Yeats is not talking theological doctrine; he is expressing a human experience. And the way in which this experience, a poignant memory of a frustrated love affair, enlarges itself into a supernatural vision is very characteristic of Yeats. One does not doubt the reality, the sweating actuality, of the poet's feeling; the poem begins in a slightly artificial and literary way, with its inversions ('That seemed as though ice burned and was but the more ice') and the faintly Biblical 'thereupon', but in the line 'And I took all the blame out of all sense and reason' it moves into the most natural and heartfelt language. This, one feels, is just how one does talk to oneself and rage at oneself at such a moment. Many poets, in fact, would have ended the poem there.

Yeats, by contrast, moves out towards the general as fast as he can. One is taken by surprise by that 'Riddled with light': the previous line, 'Until I cried and trembled and rocked to and fro' seems to be depicting ordinary human chagrin and recrimination, and then, with that 'Riddled with light', one finds oneself involved in ideas about revelation and Purgatory. The poem moves with extraordinary precipitancy; and, I suggest, it is part of its tehnical mastery that it renders so vividly, though without crude mimicry, the headlong expulsion of the ghost on to the roads—symbolizing the headlong sequence of emotions that have rushed across the poet's heart. That *enjambement* 'sent/Out naked' hurls us onwards, with held breath.

I would draw your attention to something else. Part of the power of the poem lies, I think, in the fact that Yeats has made it out of two sentences only. The complex logic of the heart and its emotions has been expressed by the logic of a complex sentence—by intricate sentences beautifully articulated in all their parts and working with absolute naturalness within the metrical structure and the rhyme structure. This handling of a complex syntax is something Yeats grew steadily more resourceful in through his career. Indeed, to tell the truth, I think he might have written this poem even better ten years later. It strikes me that 'and left but memories, that should be out of season/With the hot blood of youth, of love crossed long ago' is not quite perfectly managed: it is rather hard to speak that parenthesis 'that should be out of season/With the hot blood of youth' without destroying the onward movement of the sense. Try reading it aloud and you will see what I mean. There are too many 'of's, for one thing. However, it is a very minor flaw, if it is one at all. Still, while we are on the subject, consider the poem 'The Living Beauty' (*Collected Poems*, p. 156). Is it not rather extraordinary how its opening sentence endlessly prolongs itself and, when you think it *must* be reaching its conclusion, takes a new lease of life with the repetition of 'Appears'? There is an anecdote in Joseph Hone's biography of Yeats which reveals how much importance Yeats attached to syntax, that is to say to a muscular sentence construction in which all the parts of a sentence work for their keep and are in an active relation to one another. He was rehearsing a broadcast reading of his verse in 1937, when the reader, A. C. Clinton-Baddeley, read the first lines of 'Sailing to Byzantium':

> That is no country for old men. The young
> In one another's arms, birds in the trees . . .

Yeats exclaimed 'Stop! That is the worst bit of syntax I ever wrote', and changed it on the spot to:

> Old men should quit a country where the young
> In one another's arms, birds in the trees . . .

(though he did not adopt this alteration permanently).

❧ Let us look at another poem, 'At Galway Races', published in 1910 (*Collected Poems*, p. 108). Assuming that you like the poem (of course you may not, though I do myself, extremely), can you define why you do? As I have said earlier, the way to pin down one's feelings about a poem is to begin with a perfectly open mind—not, anyway in the first instance, to dutifully test it for 'verse movement', 'metaphors', 'ambiguities' etc. but simply to register anything whatever that catches your attention as being pleasurable or odd or characteristic. Doing this for myself, having only 'discovered' the poem recently, I noticed the curiously casual rhyme 'the course is/horses', and it struck me that its casualness might be significant. Can you see how, in this poem, it could be?

Discussion
Is not this casualness, this nonchalance, somehow akin to the quality of life that Yeats is celebrating in the poem? ❧

❧ And how would you define that quality?

Discussion
A joyful self-forgetfulness, a passionate and carefree delight in life: that might do, perhaps, as a very rough description. ❧

Another feature of the poem which struck me is its circularity. The poem revolves like the sort of song or dance called a 'round'; we come out—not knowing quite how—where we came in, picturing again those riders and cheering racecourse crowds, but this time with a larger meaning. Again there seems to be aptness in this; for the poem is talking about the inexhaustibility of nature and asserting that what one loses is not lost for ever; things come round in a circle.

What else? I am struck by the mere boldness and beauty of the comparison of a cheering racecourse to the world itself, and by the adventurous developments of this metaphor: an Earth which *sings*, as a poet sings (I suspect a distant allusion to the music of the spheres); and an Earth which has living flesh and is 'wild', as horses and men are.

I am impressed, too, by the lightness and cheerful ease with which so vast a theme, the permanent vitality of nature, can be tied to so everyday a spectacle as a horse race. There is a shock of pleasure in finding that last line, 'That ride upon horses'—a line which could not be more simple—conveying so much meaning.

❧　And what does the line mean?

Discussion

I suppose: 'Who live with self-delight, not cramped by self-consciousness and timid calculation'; also, 'Who live with a certain pride, a certain style and elevation, not plodding ingloriously along the ground.' ❧

Would it help in enjoying the poem to know more about Yeats's views upon life, politics and religion? I have to admit that it might. But what is worth remembering is that it might also hinder. For, if I guess rightly what Yeats is meaning about the 'merchant and the clerk', it is surely rather a silly view? I mean, who is Yeats, the poor relation of an Irish shipowner, to despise 'merchants'? And when was that Golden Age before there were 'merchants' and 'clerks' upon the scene? In the days of Irish legend, of Ossian and Fergus perhaps; hardly more recently.

What, however, *would* most probably help, and could not hinder, would be to know as many other Yeats poems as possible; and, in particular, to know other poems in which he uses that epithet 'wild'. The word occurs, you may remember, in 'The Cold Heaven', and also in 'Easter 1916', and in each case it has, apparently, a quite different sense. Nevertheless, for an habitual reader of Yeats, the word 'wild' sets off certain signals: he comes to recognise it as a particularly Yeatsian word, and this helps us to get inside Yeats's mind.

I have been trying to argue that we do not positively need any back-ground information to enjoy a poem by Yeats, when we read it in an anthology or when we are dipping into the *Collected Poems*. It is not necessary to know that the woman involved in 'The Cold Heaven' was Maud Gonne, whom Yeats loved unrequited for many years. Nor, in reading 'The Magi', do we need to know, what Unterecker (1959) tells us, that the Magi were for Yeats 'symbols of the inexorably cyclical movement of history'. They are facts well worth knowing, the first because we are naturally inquisitive about Yeats's life, and the second because it puts into plain words what we may have sensed half-consciously in reading the poem; but we can enjoy and possess the poem without this knowledge. Nevertheless, the more poems by Yeats we know, the more fully and precisely the meaning of any particular poem unfolds in our mind. This is, for one thing, because Yeats formed certain of his ruling ideas very early on in his career and spent a lifetime in meditating upon them. That is probably true of most poets, but it was especially true of Yeats; he was amazed, himself, on re-reading his early work late in life, to find how bitterly, as a young man of twenty or so, he was already raging against the 'injustice' of age and decay—a theme from which he made some of his finest poetry as an ageing man. Likewise, certain traditional symbols—for instance, shall we say, the swan—served him in a succession of poems; and just because he was a poet who did *not* repeat himself, he assumed—very reasonably—that his readers might remember earlier poems of his in which such symbols occurred and the kind of personal meaning he had previously given to them. Thus, if we want to understand the sym-bolism of a given poem, the best place to look for help is in his other poems, especially other poems in the same volume of verse.

An important point to remember is that, with Yeats, the important unit is not so much the single poem as the book. Not only do the poems in a given volume illuminate one another, the volume as a whole will be found to have a meaning above and beyond that of the poems com-posing it. Accordingly I plan next to study two of Yeats's volumes as a whole, choosing for this purpose *The Wind Among the Reeds* (1899), which is the perfect flowering of his 'Celtic Twilight' period; and *The Tower* (1928), as being possibly his greatest achievement.

The Wind Among the Reeds (1899)

The Wind Among The Reeds is not a very lengthy collection, so I would like you to make yourself fairly familiar with it. It would be worth spending quite a time on this, till you have a good grasp of the broad design of the volume and of the way one group of poems follows another. (You should also look at Yeats's notes to the volume in *Collected Poems*, pp. 524–529.)

❧ Assuming that you have done this, I propose to approach the poems in the opposite way from the one used so far: instead of focusing on particular poems and working out from them to a general sense of Yeats's purposes, let us start by considering the volume in its entirety. Does it, to begin with, seem to you to have a central subject?

Discussion
Well, I suppose one could say, without much fear of contradiction, that it is about unhappiness in love. ❧

❧ And why is it called *The Wind Among The Reeds*? Is it a meaningful title?

Discussion
That is not so easy to answer. ❧

❧ But which poem refers most directly to this title?

Discussion
Presumably 'He Hears the Cry of the Sedge', in which there *is* a wind crying among the reeds—telling the lover that not till the end of the world will he be allowed to lie in his beloved's arms. And, since that seems to be what, in some sense, much of the whole volume is saying, the title is surely significant?

What the wind is saying, though, is ambiguous. It could mean 'You are never going to enjoy your beloved'—as one might say, brutally,

'Poor chap, you'll never be as lucky as that, not till doomsday.' Or it could mean that there is some point in the poet's trying to imagine the end of the world and the winding up of the Universe. In fact, as we perceive from reading the other poems, it must mean both; for there are a number of poems evoking apocalyptic visions—visions of Armageddon or some Last Battle or of the dismantling of the Universe. ❧

❧   Just to refresh your memory, which are they?

Discussion

Most obviously: 'He mourns for the Change that has come upon Him and his Beloved and longs for the the End of the World', 'He remembers forgotten Beauty', 'The Valley of the Black Pig', and 'The Secret Rose'; though the theme is referred to in other poems as well. ❧

We next have to ask ourselves in what spirit the poet strives to imagine the end of the world. However, before this, we should consider the date of the collection, 1899: for it is that of the end of the nineteenth century. People have always found the end of a century significant: it is a moment which always produces prophecies and chiliastic speculations, visions of the end of the world and the like. Of course, much of this is purely cranky; but such apocalyptic feelings seem to have been intense at the end of the nineteenth century and not just among cranks. The term *fin de siècle* ('end of the century'), a name applied to the poets of the late 1880s and 1890s, contained some implication that Western culture was nearing its end like that of the late Roman empire. Mallarmé, too, said, in words often quoted by Yeats, that the air of that period was disturbed by 'the trembling of the veil of the Temple'; the age was on the verge of some unimagined revelation, it was seeking to bring forth a 'sacred book'. And then there was the further fact that Europe was full of anticipations of war. Yeats recalls that, at the end of the century, mediums and clairvoyants all over the world were prophesying war (*Autobiographies*, p. 336); and his own friend MacGregor Mathers, in the Order of the Golden Dawn, was announcing 'the imminence of immense wars'. Mathers, Yeats thought, might have given him the germ of his poem 'The Valley of the Black Pig'.

   Thus we should probably think of the 'wind among the reeds' as signifying—as one might put it—'a rumour of great changes': this indeed is how the phrase rings in our ears as we study the volume. A further important hint, though, is given by Yeats in his notes to the poems (*Collected Poems*, pp. 524–529). He says there that the Sidhe or Fairy Host, which figure in the opening poem, are associated in Irish legend with the wind. This 'host', or army of supernatural beings, appears, likewise, in a number of the poems: particularly 'The Host of the Air'. 'The Unappeasable Host' and 'He Bids his Beloved be at Peace'.

What I think we are to infer from this is that the armies of Armageddon are not only a vision of the future but a present alternative for the lover. He hears the 'host' calling to him, like a crying of the wind among the reeds: urging him to leave ordinary mortal life, with its pleasures and sorrows, its hopes, affections and fears, and join their immortal and inhuman band. As a mortal he is suffering and weak, his heart a prey to the chagrins of love; as an immortal he would enjoy an inhuman and joyous energy.

This brings me to a further point of information: it seems likely that behind *The Wind Among The Reeds* there lies Yeats's recollections of Shelley's famous 'Ode to the West Wind', where the wind, blowing through the world, is hailed both as 'Destroyer' and 'Preserver'. You might like to look the poem up (it is in innumerable anthologies) for it gives one a sense of Yeats's relationship to the Romantic movement.

Returning to that fairy 'host' in *The Wind Among The Reeds*, one can tell, I think, that the kind of alternative it offers to ordinary suffering human existence is very vivid to Yeats. That opening poem, 'The Hosting of the Sidhe', is surely full of imaginative energy: the poet's spirits rise at the invitation to 'come away', to 'Empty your heart of its mortal dream'. There is a boisterousness and glee in the imagined experience: life might well be lost for this, is the suggestion. The same is true of 'The Unappeasable Host': the poet thrills to his own vision of the gay, ruthless 'Danaan children'* with their pagan invitation. Humble mortal life, with its simple Catholic pieties and imminent grave, is made to seem a poor rival to wild and heathen freedom.

A further point of information is needed here. The early readers of 'The Hosting of the Sidhe' would most likely have read Yeats's first long poem, 'The Wanderings of Oisin'. (It is printed on pp. 409–447 of *Collected Poems*.) In this the hero, Oisin, is enticed away for three hundred years to the fairy world by the goddess Niamh. He first visits the island of Aengus, the Country of the Young, where he spends his days in revelry and dancing; then a second island, where he acts the knight errant and battles daily with a demon; then finally the Island of Forgetfulness where he enjoys a lotus-eating oblivion. Eventually, however, the remembrance of his old comrades, the heroic race of the Fenians, makes him regretfully decide he must return from these immortal regions to his native Ireland. He finds everything there diminished and unheroic: his companions are dead, the old gods are

---

* As Yeats explains in his notes, the 'Danaans', the tribes of the goddess Dana, are the ancient gods of Ireland, reduced in later days to the status of fairies.

worshipped no longer, and the land is covered with little bell-ringing Christian chapels.

One meaning of this poem must be, crudely, that a poet might be happier living the imaginative life, pure and simple: he brings himself down to the real world, with its pains and duties, reluctantly. It is the theme of many late-Romantic poems (for instance Matthew Arnold's 'The Scholar Gipsy'), and by the time of *The Wind Among The Reeds* Yeats had moved beyond it and had more complex things to say. I bring it in here because it helps explain what Niamh in 'The Hosting of the Sidhe' is calling the poet to, when she cries 'Away, come away'. (If you are curious, it will not be a waste of your time to read 'The Wanderings of Oisin', which contains some magnificent passages.)

Continuing this general survey of the volume's themes: one more *motif* to consider in *The Wind Among The Reeds* is *twilight*. Twilight and dawn, the hushed times of dewfall and moths, feature in many of the poems; and one might put this down as simply romantically 'poetic', but I think it has a more specific meaning. One should remember that the Celtic literary movement of the 1890s came to be known as 'The Celtic Twilight'. The name was invented by Yeats himself, who, in 1893, published a volume of tales called *The Celtic Twilight*.* In a story† published in *The Secret Rose* (1897), he has this sentence:

> . . . day by day as he wandered slowly and aimlessly he passed deeper and deeper into that Celtic twilight in which heaven and earth so mingle that each seems to have taken upon itself some shadow of the other's beauty.

He says, too, in the dedication to *The Secret Rose*: 'They [the stories in this volume] have but one subject, the war of spiritual with natural order.' Thus, twilight and dawn, in his imagination, seem to stand for the borderland where this-wordly and other-worldly things merge, or the frontier where they come into conflict.

❧ In reading the poem 'Into the Twilight' (*Collected Poems*, pp. 65–66) you will probably have guessed at this implication of twilight. But let us ponder on this poem for a moment. It is a rather paradoxical one, isn't it—for instance its third line? Where does the paradox lie?

Discussion

Well, grey twilight seems a surprising time or place to *laugh* in. The paradox must be deliberate, for it runs through the poem. The

---

* Available, in a revised version, in *Mythologies* (1962), Macmillan, Basingstoke.
† 'The Twisting of the Rope and Hanrahan the Red'.

meaning is that the heart, wearied by the age (the Victorian age?) that it lives in, is to seek fresh vigour and vitality in things seemingly ghostly, grey and shadowy. This was in fact the central belief of the 'Nineties movement that Yeats represented. It held that to escape from the brash, bustling, materialistic Victorian age, the artist had to resort to the dim, arcane and shadowy. It was here that, unsuspected by journalists and politicians, the permanent energies of the human spirit lay. For Yeats it was here, too, that the hopes of the Irish nation— 'Your mother Eire'—lay; it lay in that 'nationwide multiform reverie'* which would unite the Irish as a race. And to find the energies, one needed to escape the 'nets of wrong and right'—that is to say, or so I interpret it, to penetrate beyond ethics and didacticism and well-meaning debate about duty and social progress, into the deeper regions of the psyche.

All this is not to deny that 'Into the Twilight' is an exceedingly langourous, dreamy, and perhaps slightly sentimental poem. I do not consider it one of the best in the volume and would not object if someone called it 'dated'. My point is that it is not just an 'escapist' poem but expresses a challenging theory, a theory of which there are echoes throughout the volume. ❧

But if the volume, as we agreed (at least I suppose we did) is about unhappy love, what is the connection between this and its apocalyptic visions: visions of the end of the world and of gay, ruthless, supernatural 'hosts' coursing among men unseen?

I suggest that the lover is saying to his mistress: 'See what you drive me to. You make me long for the end of the world. You make me want to escape from the human race.' That is to say, there is a good deal of irony involved in those visions: the poet is making himself out as a crazed and desperate man, and saying 'What alternative do you offer me to being crazed and desperate?' The volume is, to a great degree, a complaint against love. For all that the poet is deeply in love, he rarely says anything tender to his mistress. The tenderest poem, I would say, is 'The Lover mourns for the Loss of love', where, as you will perceive, the tenderness is all for another woman.

It is a touching poem, wouldn't you agree? And it exemplifies what I said earlier about Yeats being a traditional poet: there is no absolutely obvious reason why Shelley or Byron might not have written it, though at the same time there is nothing in the least imitative about it. It is not till one knows Yeats well that one senses something peculiar to him in the lines 'She looked in my heart one day/And saw your image was there'. Yeats, with his researches into magic and the occult, attached a rather specific and magical meaning to 'images', and I

* He uses this phrase in *Autobiographies*, p. 263.

MR W B YEATS. PRESENTING MR GEORGE MOORE TO THE QUEEN OF THE FAIRIES.

Mr W. B. Yeats presenting Mr George Moore to the Queen of the Fairies by Max Beerbohm. (Max Beerbohm, 1904, *Poets Corner*, Heinemann)

think this meaning may be lurking in the lines; but if so, it is not important. Nor is it important to know that the poem is based on a real incident: a love affair with a married woman, Olivia Shakespeare,* which came to a sudden end when she realised Yeats was still hopelessly in love with Maud Gonne. What is more important, or anyhow would be satisfying, is to know why that last line 'She has gone weeping away', is so poignant and beautiful (if you agree that it is). I think that there may be a clue in the fact that Yeats shifts suddenly from the 'past historic' tense ('dreamed', 'looked'), which appears to place the event in the past—it could be twenty years ago—to the 'perfect' tense 'she has gone'), which reveals that it has just happened. The point of speaking as though it were in the indefinite past seems to be to imply: 'My love for you is so fatal and all-consuming that this other love affair of mine, which it has just wrecked, already seems to belong to the distant past.'

Do we find Yeats using masks in this volume (see pp. 17–19 above on 'Masks and Anti-selves')? I think that we do, and that they and the irony I have spoken of are related. Aengus, in 'The Song of Wandering Aengus', seems to be a (light-hearted) disguise or masks for Yeats as a crazed lover, ruining his life for a phantasm. The poet in 'He wishes for the Cloths of Heaven' is, again light-heartedly, a caricature of the Romantic poet and lover, the long-haired dreamy poet of bad sentimental novels. The poem has become an anthology piece—rightly, because it is very charming—but it is in a sense a joke of Yeats's at his own expense. These cheerful masks counterbalance the bitterer irony—if I am right in finding it irony—of his visionary and apocalyptic poems.

If one looks for poems that seem to express Yeat's feelings directly, without the disguise of a mask, the nearest one can find are perhaps 'He thinks of Those who have spoken Evil of his Beloved', and 'He thinks of his Past Greatness when a Part of the Constellation of Heaven': one a boast, or confident assertion of his genius, and the other a complaint against sexual frustration. They are neither of them about Romantic love. Romantic or ideal love seems throughout to be submitted to irony and complicated criticism. The poet's repeated entreaties to his mistress to cover him with her hair begin to sound ironic and sinister, as though it were a kind of death he were demanding. Again, in 'The Cap and Bells', the point appears to be that the beloved woman is not satisfied until she has robbed the jester not only of his heart and his soul but of his very professional *raison d'être*, his cap and bells. (Translating this into real life, it would mean that the poet's mistress would like him to sacrifice to her not only his feelings

---

* She remained a lifelong friend of Yeats's, and her daughter Dorothy married Ezra Pound.

and mind but his very poetic gift itself.) Receiving that as a gift, she is at last satisfied; she places the gift in her bosom, 'Under a cloud of her hair' (that faintly sinister hair again!) and croons a love song to it, as Salome sang to the severed head of John the Baptist. This, in more literal terms, is an accusation that Yeats might well have brought in his heart against Maud Gonne: that, in her fanaticism, she would have liked him to give up poetry for the political activities of the Irish nationalists. (We should remember, though, that, according to Yeats's note (*Collected Poems*, p. 526), the poem came to him in a dream, and, though it always meant a great deal to him, 'as is the way with symbolical poems, it has not always meant quite the same thing'.)

Pursuing this theme of Yeats's irony, let us consider another poem, 'The Lover tells of the Rose in his Heart'. It is a lilting and lyrical poem, apparently an effusion of traditional, hyperbolical lover-like sentiment. Is there more to it than that? I suspect that if we read it in an anthology we should not think so. Here we see the advantage of studying a volume as a whole. For in the context of neighbouring poems, I think we do see more in the poem and its tone.

❧ Ask yourself: 'Are we meant to approve of these sentiments of the Lover?'

Discussion

Looking at them in cold blood, we scarcely can, surely? They are really very dubious. If being romantically in love makes us want to ignore the crying of children or the fatigue of work-worn labourers, then it cannot be a very good thing. For the Lover does not propose to succour these sufferers, he merely wants to escape to a 'green knoll' and dream of a world where no such ugly things exist. ❧

Well, of course, Yeats is allowing for these reflections of ours. Having read the rest of *The Wind Among The Reeds* we are on the lookout for irony about romantic love, and find here another example.

❧ Following the principle of scrutinizing any curious feature, any faint oddity in a poem, in case it holds significance, I pause over those last two lines:

> With the earth and the sky and the water, re-made, like a casket of gold
> For my dreams of your image that blossoms a rose in the deeps of my heart.

Do you find them strange in any way? Could you explain *precisely* what is meant with regard to that 'casket', 'dreams', 'image', 'rose' or 'heart'?

Discussion

'Casket', 'dreams', 'image', 'rose' and 'heart' do seem rather an over-abundance of things to be parcelled up together in a single metaphor. The lines remind one faintly of:

> This is the malt that lay in the house that Jack built:
> This is the rat that ate the malt that lay in the house that Jack
>   built.

a curious string of objects, each related to the next. But the implication, I suggest, is that the Lover is putting the thought of his beloved in the innermost and most inaccessible receptacle: a box within a box within a box. The thought itself is at two removes from reality, not just an 'image' but his 'dreams' of an image. And not only are these dreams hidden away in a heart; for further protection from the contaminating world, that heart is to be placed in a vast casket. Through the odd syntax of these lines Yeats 'enacts', or provides us with a model of, the Lover's fanatical effort to make his love something apart from his ordinary human existence. ✤

One reason why I have stressed, and perhaps over-stressed, the irony in *The Wind Among The Reeds*, is because irony, of a more mordant, more searching kind, becomes a leading feature in Yeats's later poetry. Thus to study it here will sharpen one's sense of the differences, but also the affinities, between the early and the late Yeats.

Thoor Ballylee, Gort, County Galway, the summer home of the Yeatses from 1919 until 1929. (Irish Tourist Board)

The Tower
(1928)

Introduction

In the *Celtic Twilight* (1893) Yeats wrote, in somewhat *fin de siècle* tones, of an ancient tower or castle at Ballylee in Galway.

> I have been lately to a little group of houses, not many enough to be called a village, in the barony of Kiltartan in County Galway, whose name, Ballylee, is known through all the west of Ireland. There is the old square castle, Ballylee, inhabited by a farmer and his wife, and a cottage where their daughter and their son-in-law live, and a little mill with an old miller, and old ash-trees throwing green shadows upon a little river and great stepping-stones . . . I have been there this summer, and I shall be there again before it is autumn, because Mary Hynes, a beautiful woman whose name is still a wonder by turf fires, died there sixty years ago; for our feet would linger where beauty has lived its life of sorrow to make us understand that it is not of this world.

Some twenty years later, this tower, which stood not far from Coole Park, was lying empty and roofless, and on an impulse Yeats bought it, for the sum of £35. He had no immediate plans for inhabiting it, but soon after his marriage the idea grew on him of repairing it and using it as a summer retreat. The process took several years, for he was still a poor man and had to pay for the repairs from occasional literary earnings; and he never intended to make it his permanent home. He was not a man who required a home, being content to live a nomadic existence in borrowed houses, and regarding friendship as a sufficient 'home'. The tower became for him, rather, a place to write in, and furthermore a symbol—a symbol of the artist's role as he liked to fancy it: that is to say, the role of a man labouring in night and solitude and thereby acquiring magical powers. This was a favourite anti-self for Yeats, who was in real life an extremely gregarious and talkative man. Some lines from Shelley's fragment 'Prince Athanase' had haunted him from early youth:

> His soul had wedded Wisdom, and her dower
> Is love and justice, clothed in which he sate
> Apart from men, as in a lonely tower

These lines became linked in his mind with some others from Milton's 'Il Penseroso':

> Or let my lamp at midnight hour,
> Be seen in some high lonely Tower,
> Where I may oft out-watch the *Bear*,
> With thrice-great *Hermes*, or unsphere
> The spirit of Plato to unfold
> What worlds, or what vast regions hold
> The immortal mind that hath forsook
> Her mansion in this fleshy nook.

His tower at Ballylee embodied for him this Shelleyan and Miltonic dream; and it also evoked ancient Ireland, for traditions clustered round such towers—for instance the local legend of that beautiful Mary Hynes and of the blind poet Raftery, last of the Irish bards, who immortalized her. Indeed, this being Yeats, a fine crop of symbols soon sprouted for him around his tower, and what had begun as a romantic fancy gradually developed into complex poetic thinking. The tower had a winding stair—plenty of symbolism there! For a spiral staircase naturally recalls the spiralling 'eternal recurrence' of history. And then, would not a tower suggest the male sexual organ and a winding stair the female one? And then again, now he comes to remember it, isn't the sixteenth card in the Tarot pack a Lightning-struck Tower? . . . I am caricaturing Yeats here, for there is something faintly comic and over-deliberate, as well as impressive, in the way he could always find grist for his symbol-mill and rejected from his life anything that could not be turned to symbolic profit. This story of his tower is intensely characteristic: he worked at his tower as he worked at his poems, and—a culminating symbol—he wanted his tower to be the physical emblem of his poetry. He told his friend Sturge Moore: 'I like to think of that building as a permanent symbol of my work, plainly visible to the passer-by. As you know, all my art theories depend upon just this—rooting of mythology in the earth'.

Very naturally, then, his tower became for him the organizing symbol for a sequence of poems, the collection named *The Tower*, this volume being followed, according to the Yeatsian principle of contraries, by a volume, *The Winding Stair* (1933), which was in some ways an 'answer' to it.

So let us look at *The Tower*, as we have looked at *The Wind Among The Reeds*, as a whole, but this time with something further in view: not merely to analyse its themes but to see if the volume has, as you might say, a 'plot', a continuous 'action' running from its beginning to its end.

The Lonely Tower: engraving by Samuel Palmer to illustrate 'Il Pensoroso'. This Palmer engraving was of particular importance to Yeats. (Crown copyright: Victoria and Albert Museum)

'SAILING TO BYZANTIUM'

The first poem, 'Sailing to Byzantium', does not draw upon the tower for its symbolism at all; it takes its metaphors or symbols from Byzantium, the 'holy city' of the Christianized Roman empire (the city we now know as Istanbul). We need to study the poem carefully, for its position as the opening poem is no accident. I suggest you read it a number of times; you might even learn it by heart.

❧   Having got the feeling of the poem, the next thing to do might be to make clear to yourself what its plot or 'action' is.

Discussion
It seems to be somewhat as follows. The speaker, being now an old man, has decided that his native country is no place for him; it is the country of the young, the country of sensual happiness and the enjoyments of the passing day, and in such a country, so he feels, an old man is a figure of fun, a mere scarecrow. He has therefore taken ship and sailed to 'the holy city of Byzantium'. There, in that religious spot, he appeals for aid to the sages standing in 'God's holy fire'. (And since the sages are 'standing' in this fire, and not consumed by it, we can reasonably guess that the fire is that of Purgatory.) He asks the sages to return to earth from Purgatory to teach his soul to 'sing' and to destroy his 'heart', his human feelings, which are now a burden to him. He tells them that, once he has escaped from the natural human world, he will take on a new body: not a flexible, perishable living body but a hard, changeless one, like that of a mechanical bird—a precious toy of gold and enamelling such as emperors employ to distract their idle hours. ❧

❧   A poem about old age, then, and what to do about old age. These are grey and banal words, but let us think what other words we could use. Is it a poem about *facing* old age?

Discussion
But that would suggest that age is simply a calamity to be faced, whereas the speaker can at least *imagine* age as victorious: the soul 'clapping its hands' and singing triumphantly, the more triumphantly the further the body decays. ❧

❧   Is it a poem about *escaping* from old age and its humiliations?

Discussion

Partly that, perhaps. But though the speaker, by taking ship, has escaped from the country of the young, he has not definitely found sanctuary: he will not be secure until his heart, his natural human feelings, have been consumed away; and this has not yet happened, as we know from his heartfelt outcries, nor is it certain it will ever happen. And say it were to happen, can an escape be also a triumph? To have one's heart consumed away seems a high price to pay, and the reward, after all, is no very high dignity if it means resembling a clockwork bird on a tree. How does that fit with the idea of victory and triumph? ❧

If we are asking what conclusion about life Yeats or the speaker is expressing, we shall not really get much further than this. Whatever formula we find for stating the poem's argument, there will always turn out to be some objection. Of course this could mean that the poem is a muddle. But it does not *sound* like a muddle. Quite the reverse, in fact: the poem strikes one as highly organized and purposeful. Thus if it does not add up to a single statement about life—such a statement as you might find, say, in a Wordsworth sonnet—this must be because it is not that sort of poem. And so what sort of poem is it? I suggest, a poem deliberately dramatizing an unending, and perhaps an unendable, argument. It expresses a process of feeling that has taken place, and will take place, in the poet's heart not once but a thousand times.

I say 'dramatizing', for this is important, clearly. Yeats has invented not merely a metaphor or symbol for his feelings towards old age but a drama—which means something not merely personal to the author. This old man and his situation is an account of Yeats's own situation only in the sense that Lear on the heath is an account of Shakespeare's. Yeats stands outside this old man, with his questionable enterprise of sailing to Byzantium, so that we are free to react to him with mixed feelings: with fellow-feeling, with pity and with a sense of his possible ridiculousness.

Apropos of this, can you suggest why Yeats did not finally adopt that amendment to the first line which he improvised when rehearsing a broadcast reading (see p. 30). I would guess, because 'That is no country for old men' emphasizes at the very start the dramatic aspect of the poem. The old man, having taken ship to Byzantium, looks back on the place he has quit, exclaiming vehemently: '*That* is no country for old men.'

You might call the process of feeling expressed by the poem a 'debate', perhaps. But if so, it is not like a normal debate. It is not like a political debate, in which one does one's level best to blacken one's opponent's arguments. It is not even like a philosophers' debate, fair-mindedly allowing a partial validity to *this* argument and a partial validity to *that* and then trying to resolve their differences. Instead, it is a debate in which each factor involved is an absolute. We are made absolutely convinced of the desirability of that country of the young: no envy is allowed to discolour that picture, so rich, so vivid, of the 'salmon-falls, the mackerel-crowded seas'—though it is precisely to avoid a degrading envy that the old man must escape. Again, we are absolutely persuaded of the possibility of triumphing over decay and senility. The assertion:

> An aged man is but a paltry thing,
> A tattered coat upon a stick, unless
> Soul clap its hands and sing, and louder sing
> For every tatter in its mortal dress

has an exultant vigour that seems much more than just defiant. And, finally, we accept absolutely the misery of the speaker's plight. Could there be more heartfelt and overwhelming lines than these:

> Consume my heart away; sick with desire
> And fastened to a dying animal
> It knows not what it is

(But notice the ambiguity here: 'sick with desire' can mean both sick *of* desire and full of intense desire.)

There should be nothing to surprise us in the fact that the poem can contain three such rival emotions. What we need to be surprised by is Yeats's feat in holding them, uncontaminated by one another, in a single act of vision, and revealing at the same time how they lead into one another. Here is one of the highest tasks poetry can perform. Yeats here, as in 'The Cold Heaven' and 'Easter 1916', is concerned with the logic of emotions, the way one emotion develops logically into another or into its contrary; and the logic of his syntax, and of the progression of his stanzas, is an expression of this logic of the heart.

❧   It is, of necessity, a subtle and difficult logic, and the final lines of 'Sailing to Byzantium' are deeply ambiguous. What do you make of that phrase 'the artifice of eternity' ('gather me/Into the artifice of eternity')?

Discussion

It must mean, partly, 'Give to me, poor, ageing, confused animal, the fixity and freedom from change and human passion of a work of art.' It is a thought not too remote from Keats's in his 'Ode on a Grecian Urn', where Keats contrasts the fate of the lovers depicted on the urn with that of human lovers: a bitter fate, in that they can never kiss, but a happy fate in that they can never grow old or suffer satiety.

However, we also detect irony: for one sense of 'artifice', after all, is *trick*, a ruse or device. And it must be one of the poet's thoughts that there may be no real escape from the human condition—any escape must be a kind of wilful pretence. And, reading the final stanza, we find that the kind of 'eternal' work of art the speaker has in mind is, appropriately, nothing so dignified as a Grecian urn; it is a clockwork bird, an artificial toy built to amuse a bored emperor.

There is a further implication, however, which is that, though any attempt to escape from the human condition must be an 'artifice', and 'heavens' and 'eternities' are made up not by God but by man—they are constructed by an act of the human will—this does not make these eternities any less real. (This theme is stated more clearly in the next poem, 'The Tower', but I think it is present in 'Sailing to Byzantium' and is hinted at obliquely in the fact that the speaker does not intend, like some Hindu or Buddhist, to leave it to fate or his *karma* to decide what shape he shall take in his next incarnation: he is going to choose the shape for himself.)

This ambiguous attitude implied in the word 'artifice' is important in the poem and is continued in the final stanza, and especially in the last line of all. One can think of the clockwork bird as truly prophetic: the speaker, by renouncing his ordinary humanity, has in exchange acquired supernatural powers and can speak clairvoyantly of 'what is past, or passing, or to come'. But another possible meaning of this singing of 'what is past, or passing, or to come' might be merely 'court gossip'—something like what the imprisoned King Lear describes to Cordelia:

> . . . so we'll live,
> And pray, and sing, and tell old tales, and laugh
> At gilded butterfles, and hear poor rogues
> Talk of court news; and we'll talk with them too—
> Who loses and who wins; who's in, who's out—

These are very deep ironies, inescapable ironies in the very nature of existence, that Yeats is exploring. An old man, trying to find some compensation for the youth that he has lost is in some aspects bound to be a figure of fun, and a pretension to supernatural or prophetic powers as a compensation for natural ones cannot but have its dubious, possibly ridiculous, side. But then, the whole situation of man, inventing heavens and theologies for himself and then believing in them, is from some points of view ridiculous. ❧

Notice, by the way, the family likeness between the ironies and paradoxes he is expressing here and those that he was exploring thirty years before in regard to the Romantic lover or the losses and gains involved in being a poet at all: the tug-of-war between being a poet and being a human being.

You might also, at this point, look again at what I said about Yeats and the mask. His theory of life as proceeding by contraries and of art as 'an intellectual daily re-creation of all that exterior fate snatches away' has much relevance to 'Sailing to Byzantium' and to all of this volume.

I have spent a lot of time on this poem, but let me just add one or two haphazard remarks.

❧ Does the phrase, 'Fish, flesh, or fowl' carry any particular overtone for you?

Discussion

It reminds me of the phrase 'Flesh, fowl, or good red herring'; and this kind of unobtrusive nod towards a proverbial expression seems to me very Yeatsian. It is one of the means by which his style, though elevated in diction, keeps its feet on the ground. (There is something similar in the phrase in 'At Galway Races': 'Hearing the whole world change its tune'. We are meant just faintly to recall the slang usage of the phrase, as when we say of somebody 'He soon changed his tune', i.e. began to talk with a different attitude. ❧

❧ What sense are we to make of the phrase 'perne in a gyre' in stanza 3?

Discussion

It is the one genuinely obscure phrase in the poem. Yeats has provided a clue to 'perne' in his note on the poem 'Shepherd and Goatherd' (see *Collected Poems*, p. 531), where he explains that it is another name for a spool, such as thread is wound on. And a 'gyre' is, of course, a circle or spiral. Thus, assuming that 'perne' is here used as a verb rather than a noun, the meaning seems to be: 'Retrace (i.e., unwind) the stages of your existence': return to Earth from Purgatory, in order to teach my soul to 'sing'. ❧

'Gyres' and 'perning in a gyre' have a complicated significance for Yeats.* He had a theory, expounded in 'A Vision' (see Appendix II)

---

* 'Pern' is also the name of a kind of hawk, and, as T. R. Henn remarks in *The Lonely Tower*, pp. 185–186, ' "gyre" and "perne" are also associated with bird-flight, and the failure of the falconer, God, to control the falcon, the human mind in its spiral ascent'.

and drawn on frequently in the present volume, of history as a matter of one age unwinding what another age has wound, and he also had a notion of a man at his death unwinding the stages of his life. However, these ideas hardly seem relevant in the present context; and I have some sympathy with F. R. Leavis, who finds Yeats's phrase here a blot, an unnecessary difficulty. He says:

> When I first read the poem the *New English Dictionary* didn't help me with 'perne' ('Perne in a gyre'), but I wasn't seriously troubled; the poetic context charged the word sufficiently for its function. Now that I *know* what 'perne' literally means the poem has gained nothing. On the contrary, not only would the pre-Yeatsian meaning be a nuisance in itself if thought of; the loaded 'perne' added to 'gyre' makes it more difficult for the reader to repress the movement of irritation aroused in him by the Yeatsian technicality of the phrase, which stands out from the poem, and proposes another context. (Leavis, 1969).

❧   Apart from this, the only lines that do not seem perfectly clear are 'Nor is there singing school but studying/Monuments of its own magnificence'. Would you like to jot down your interpretation or paraphrase?

Discussion

Yeats's thought is certainly very condensed here. But first let us make as sure as we can of the literal sense. This is, I suggest: 'And the only way for a soul to learn to "sing" is by studying what the spirit of man (artists, thinkers, civilizations) has achieved in earlier ages—for instance this very "holy city of Byzantium", with its magnificent religious art, those "gold mosaics" for which Byzantine art is famous.'

As for the larger sense (i.e., *why* this is the only way for a soul to learn to 'sing') it relates to what we mentioned earlier: I mean, Yeats's view that though heaven, eternity and the ideal are real, man, not God, has created them, and in revering them he is, in a sense, revering himself—studying 'monuments' of his own 'magnificence'. ❧

'THE TOWER'

Now let us turn to the next poem, 'The Tower'. Yeats—or we ought rather to say 'the poet'—is now speaking in his own person, and he expands the complaint against age of 'Sailing to Byzantium' in a more direct and conversational way. The poet says that, though he never felt more creative, more full of irrepressible imagination, he will have to give up verse ('bid the Muse go pack') and occupy himself with abstract thought ('choose Plato and Plotinus for a friend'). For to be a poet one has to write from the heart, from the feelings of the natural man, and he can no longer bear the feelings of his heart: the frustrations of an ageing body make them too bitter. The sentiments are much the same as those of 'Sailing to Byzantium', with this addition, that, he says, he must not only quit the country of the young, he must quit poetry.

❧   With Section II we have what appears to be a brusque change of direction. However, if you will re-read Section I, you will see the connection of thought, quite a definite and logical connection though Yeats has not spelled it out. Section II is in some sense an answer to Section I. Can you see what I mean?

Discussion
Section I may have been a cry of distress, but it was also a boast: he claimed never to have had a more 'Excited, passionate, fantastical/Imagination' than now in old age. Now in Section II he depicts that imagination at work, summoning up 'Images and memories' from the scene around him in a masterful way, almost like a necromancer raising 'spirits'. (We of course remember Yeats's occult experiments.) This connection of thought is simple and obvious enough but it is important not to miss it. Many of the longer poems in *The Tower* depend on our perceiving such connections.   ❧

The first of the images and memories the poet summons up are the arrogant Mrs French; the peasant beauty Mary Hynes and the blind poet Raftery who celebrated her; and Hanrahan, a character in some early stories of Yeats's, *Stories of Red Hanrahan*,* who is put under a spell by an old man, during a card game, and sent plunging across the fields in the moonlight in mad pursuit of a phantom quarry. (See Yeats's own note on p. 532 of *Collected Poems*.)

❧   Can you see what human quality these three 'images' or 'memories' have in common?

Discussion
They are all cases of madness: mad aristocratic arrogance on the part of Mrs French, mad and deluded quests in the case of the bewitched farmers and bewitched Hanrahan. The point is brought home by Yeats, when he says 'For if I triumph I must make men mad' and

---

* They are reprinted in *Mythologies*.

prays that the prosaic light of day and the bewildering light of the moon shall be confused in 'One inextricable beam'. ♣

♣   Will you now re-read the whole poem and try to work out what the poet means about himself when he says 'For if I triumph I must make men mad'?

Discussion

He seems to be saying that his 'Excited, passionate, fantastical' imagination, and poetic imagination generally, is not just a harmless, innocent faculty; it is a way of deluding men's wits, including his own. It is a form of intoxication and self-intoxication which is at least potentially dangerous. Thus, if he has to give up poetry, as Section I affirmed, then after all there may be something to be said for doing so. ♣

Notice the bold and surprising stroke in stanza 8 of Section II. Yeats (or the imaginary Yeats who is speaking in the poem) is letting his imagination run in its favourite channels, recreating old fictions and fantasies of his ('I thought it all out twenty years ago') and then suddenly he loses patience with himself and all that Celtic mythologizing of his youth:

> And followed up those baying creatures towards—
>
> O towards I have forgotten what—enough!

Poetry and mythologizing, or at any rate his own brand, are not only a dubious self-intoxication, they also sometimes seem futile. What *was* the end of that story about Red Hanrahan? No really! he can't be bothered to remember.

This brilliant dramatic stroke would have been beyond the scope of Yeats at the time of *The Wind Among The Reeds* (as indeed would the whole intricate structure of this poem). It is a good illustration of what he said in that letter to his father in 1913 (see p. 13):

> . . . of recent years . . . I have tried for more self-portraiture, I have tried to make my work convincing with a speech so natural that the hearer would feel the presence of a man thinking and feeling.

Yeats is undertaking self-portraiture in this poem, and furthermore is reassessing his whole life and career. He is not merely summoning up 'images' and 'memories'; he is conducting an argument with himself about his life.

There follows a curious transition; and to tell the truth I am not quite sure if it works. The poet says that why he has summoned up these phantoms is to ask them if all of them, like him, had raged against the humiliation of old age—and from the expression in their eyes he sees the answer is 'Yes'. Just for a moment, to my ear, the complex (and, surely, most impressive?) structure of the poem creaks. He needed to get back to the subject of old age, but has not quite prepared the way sufficiently: what have Mrs French and the rest to do with old age? See if you agree with me; I may have missed something.

Having put his question about old age, he dismisses all the phantoms but one, Red Hanrahan, and he asks the lecherous Hanrahan a further question. It is a question put with extraordinary subtlety. In itself it is a very simple question:

> Does the imagination dwell the most
> Upon a woman won or woman lost?

but it would take many words to draw out all the complexities of the way it is presented and the way this is linked with the rest of the poem. I will mention just one. When the poet says to Hanrahan:

> For it is certain that you have
> Reckoned up every unforeknown, unseeing
> Plunge, lured by a softening eye . . .

we are meant, presumably, to remember how Hanrahan was 'lured' by an old ruffian into 'plunging' about the countryside in pursuit of a phantom hare. Thus, winning a woman is likened to a grotesque and drunken episode. As so often with Yeats, the opposition he is presenting is very evenly balanced—as such oppositions are in life. Winning a woman can be seen as bemusing, blinding, labyrinthine and confusing; losing a woman means endless bitter self-recrimination; and both obsess the imagination. There hardly seems much to choose between them.

The poet has declared his plight (Section I). He has questioned the stages of his life which have led to this plight (Section II). He now, in Section III, makes his dispositions for the future; he draws up a will. And having made his will—it is a most powerful and unexpected idea, surely?—he imagines this will actually being executed. He pictures in imagination the process of stripping himself of all that he has accumulated in life—which in his case is not material possessions but moral qualities, such as 'pride' and 'faith'. To sail to Byzantium (for Yeats certainly means us to have that earlier poem in our thoughts) means 'dying' as regards one's preceding life; and this is precisely what is exemplified in the last lines of this present poem ('Now shall I make my soul' etc.)

I have deliberately been stressing Yeats's ideas in this analysis. It is often said that ideas do not matter, as such, in poetry. When the painter Degas complained to Mallarmé: 'I've wasted a whole day on a damned sonnet, and haven't got an inch further, and yet it isn't as if I didn't have ideas . . .', Mallarmé replied 'You don't make poems out of ideas. You make them out of words.' There is a truth in this; but one should be clear what one is meaning by 'ideas'. Yeats's views or theories about politics or the afterlife are one thing, and one need not worry too much whether one accepts them (they are sometimes very profound and sometimes rather silly, to my mind). His poetic 'ideas' or 'thought', however,—for instance such an idea as the one I have just been discussing—are quite another matter. Hearing Yeats speak about bequeathing his 'faith' and 'pride' to young men, one might think it a vague cliché, suitable to an end-of-term speech; but when he goes on to imagine the actual process of parting from these qualities, one sits up, one recognises a most original and profound idea. Appreciating his 'ideas' in this sense is not only relevant, it is, obviously, most important. The key to the whole question, and to poetry in general, is pleasure. Yeats's ideas for poems, and the ideas in his poems, often give us a shock of pleasure when they sink in upon us, and it is when they do so that we know the ideas are integral to the poetry.

Those concluding lines, 'Now shall I make my soul . . .' are some of my favourites in all twentieth-century poetry. They strike a note not sounded in 'Sailing to Byzantium'. The old man in 'Sailing to Byzantium' feels (or at any rate is tempted to feel) envy of the young, misery at his own condition, and a proud determination to change his condition. The author of 'The Tower' feels, as well as all these things, a warm bond with the life that he is quitting. If we have guessed already that the author of 'Sailing to Byzantium', unlike its hero, is not a misanthrope—he is not really saying 'Far better to be without human feelings, like a clockwork bird on a golden tree—these lines in 'The Tower' confirm it. There could not be a more tender farewell to life. It appears, after all that it is not bodily decay that is for him the worst evil, it is the death of friends and 'death/Of every brilliant eye/That made a catch in the breath'.

How these lines manage to make their effect is partly a matter of rhythm—rhythm played off against sentence construction. Notice, for instance, the break in sense which occurs, and makes a halt in the rhythm, at 'Seem but the clouds of the sky'. The crescendo of rhythm and crescendo of feeling in the preceding three lines:

> The death of friends, or death
> Of every brilliant eye
> That made a catch in the breath—

is broken, and the poem ends on a falling cadence, intensely expressive of that tranquil 'dying to life' that is being rendered. (I wonder, even, if it is not deliberate that the words 'made a catch in the breath' are followed by a literal catch in the breath on the reader's part?)

'MEDITATIONS IN TIME OF CIVIL WAR'

✿   In the three sections of 'The Tower' we have a statement, a counter-statement, and a third statement generated by the other two. You might, especially if you were a Marxist, call this a 'dialectical' progress: thesis, followed by an antithesis, followed by a synthesis. The first three sections of 'Meditations in Time of Civil War' seem to me to work in a similar way, and when you have read the poem once or twice I would like you to re-read those first three sections and identify the general train of argument; that is to say, ask yourself what the connection of thought is between 'Ancestral Houses', 'My House', and 'My Table'. It is a simple enough connection, but Yeats has not spelt it out in so many words.

Discussion

Yeats, in the first section, evokes the leisured existence of an ancestral country house: a house such as Coole Park, property of rich men and women through many generations. Amid such surroundings he asks himself, could one not live spontaneously and freely and realise oneself to the full without the need for laborious effort and self-discipline?

In Section II, 'My House', he evokes, in turn, the poet's own house; that bare, bleak tower, surrounded not by landscaped gardens and well-groomed lawns but by stony ground and ragged trees, where he, the poet, works with effort and in solitude, cultivating not the natural life (as he pictures the leisured rich as doing) but supernatural or magical powers. He has chosen to live there and identify his life with that inhospitable tower, he says, so that he can leave to his descendants, for their guidance, a symbol of 'adversity'—a symbol of that strenuous, painful life which is the opposite of that lived in 'ancestral houses'.

The antithesis of these two sections turns, partly, on two contrasting ideas about inheritance. Already in Section I, having evoked an ideal picture of the life of the leisured class, he has cast a doubt upon this picture. *Can* self-delight and sweetness in life be passed on from generation to generation? Maybe the sweetness is only a dream. It may be that ancestral houses are merely the compensating dream of sweetness, translated into brick and stone, nursed by passionate and violent men of action. Their meaning lies, according to the Yeatsian principle of contraries, in their contrast with the actual lives of their owners, and in the pampered descendants of these violent men the 'sweetness' will become mere cosiness and tameness. So, after all, the poet's tower, a symbol not of sweetness but of endurance and painful toil, may be the more lasting and real heritage.

I have said 'obeying the Yeatsian principle of contraries'. But I hope this does not imply that the principle is some arbitrary figment of Yeats's mind, some hobby-horse we have to humour him in. Surely this idea of his about ancestral houses is a profound thought, a profoundly *interesting* thought, and one that immediately comes home to us?

I have only dealt with the most obvious way in which Section II is an 'answer' to Section I. There are many other contrasts and connections between the two. For instance, the poet imagines the leisured rich as existing self-sufficiently, living from 'life's own self-delight', and he pictures the solitary scholar-artist as self-sufficient too, though in an entirely different way: in those rather condensed lines 'shadowing forth/How the daemonic rage/Imagined everything' he is representing him as being, in some magical or god-like way, the actual creator of everything that goes on round him. This is of course a poetic fancy, but it shades into more serious beliefs, such as those entertained in 'The Tower':

> Death and life were not
> Till man made up the whole,
> Made lock, stock and barrel
> Out of his bitter soul,
> Aye, sun and moon and star, all

Let us move on to Section III, 'My Table'. On the poet's bare trestle-table there lies a Japanese sword, wrapped in embroidered silk; and, prompted by this, he meditates once again about *inheritance*. In medieval Japan, so he has read, arts were handed down from father to son over many centuries; and 'soul's beauty'—beauty such as that of great art, won by toil and painful self-discipline—was prized so highly that even the leisured rich felt its claims. For all their fine clothes and social prestige their minds were 'awake'; they did not live in oblivious self-delight as the poet has pictured the dwellers in ancestral houses.

Thus Section III resolves the opposition proposed in Section I and Section II. Self-delighting life and self-denying life do not, after all, exclude each other. Yeats puts his point epigrammatically in the concluding lines of Section III: 'it seemed/Juno's peacock screamed'. ❧

❧ What do these lines mean? At a first reading they hold one up: we say to ourselves, 'Oh dear, Yeats is being obscure and allusive. I'll need to look at the Classical Dictionary and find out about Juno and peacocks, before I can make sense of this.' Not so, though. One merely has to think of what has gone before in the poem. Do you see what I mean?

Discussion

Yeats has used a bust (or garden ornament) of Juno, and peacocks straying on old terraces, as emblems of leisured country-house existence. Now, speaking of the Japanese grandee who, despite his cosseted existence and fine clothes, has an 'aching heart', he says that it is as if the peacock, with his fine feathers and stately walk, should startle us by screaming (as of course peacocks do, in a particularly harsh and grating voice). Yeats's metaphor springs quite naturally and with beautiful economy out of what has gone before; and when we verify that peacocks *are* traditionally associated with Juno it does not add very much. ❧

❧ Will you now once again re-read Section I of 'Meditations in Time of Civil War' and ask yourself how you would describe the 'feel' and texture of the *verse* of this section?

Discussion

The epithets that spring to my lips are 'supple', 'rich', 'harmonious'. I would say that it was graceful as an athlete is graceful, performing muscular feats without apparent effort. It is also, for Yeats, unusually pictorial and evocative of the physical scene: 'Amid the rustle of his planted hills' brings those wooded and 'landscaped' slopes very solidly and vividly before us. But I come back to 'athletic'. Yeats, in *A Vision*, speaks of the Byzantine mosaic-worker as bringing the supernatural before us, by his art, 'as a lovely flexible presence like that of a perfect human body'. The words seem an excellent description of these opening lines of 'Meditations in Time of Civil War'. ❧

❧ If this is their effect on us, why would that be appropriate?

Discussion

Well, because Yeats is evoking a spontaneous and natural, though ordered, life—a life lived harmoniously and without stress and inner conflict. ❧

❧ And the verse movement of Section II? How would you describe that?

Discussion

It is, surely, brusque, staccato and uncompromising, with none of those long, sinuous, beautifully proportioned sentences that wind their way around the stanza form in Section I. And this is appropriate too. ❧

Section III has again its own characteristic movement, less easy to define. (Of course, these contrasts are made with discreetness and decorum; they are not violent contrasts as in Eliot's *The Waste Land*. Yeats, as I have said, has a 'style' and makes his effects within that style; see above, p. 20.)

❧   But notice something striking: Section IV, in which the poet is again speaking about his tower, is in the same harmonious, ample style as Section I, which is about ancestral houses. Could it be that Yeats is making some particular point by this? Can you make a suggestion?

Discussion

Would it not be that the poet is now saying, partly by means of this very device, that the rugged tower—the inheritance, emblematic of toil and self-discipline, that he has prepared for his descendants—is not merely the opposite of luxurious mansions and well-tended lawns, it can also be thought *like* them (in being, like them, a substantial and 'enduring' monument). Here is another, unexpected, way in which Yeats has discreetly linked the parts of his poem together. ❧

I have not yet even mentioned the Irish Civil War. This war* and its impact on Yeats—though we do not discover the fact till Section V— are what the poem is 'about', in the ordinary sense. I shall have to cut my discussion short here: but let me just briefly outline the train of thought. When soldiers from both sides in the civil war, an 'irregular' of the Republican side and a lieutenant of the National Army, come by the poet's door, his first emotion is a pang of envy: he too would have liked to be a man of action, not a sedentary poet: a man of action like the founders of ancestral houses, or even such as that obscure man-at-arms who once occupied his tower. Then in Section VI, which is in part an answer to Section V, the poet reflects on himself, as a one-time Irish nationalist, and on the Irish in general, now engaged in con-fused and fratricidal bloodshed—of both of whom it might be said, in various senses, that their 'wall' is crumbling. The section is so mellifluous and song-like, one feels it must be saying something simple, but actually an enormous amount is compressed here, and the sense takes some trouble to disentangle: one wonders at first what the starlings have to do with the bees. What is involved must be, partly, a contrast between the parental care of the starlings and the fratricidal

---

* It would be a good idea to refresh your memory of events in Ireland in the period 1916–1924, at least in their main outlines. The account in any standard encyclopaedia would probably do for the purpose; see also the histories listed in Further Reading, p. 98.

and infanticidal cruelty of the Irish—in which accusation the poet includes himself; for he and his friends have fed their hearts not on wholesome food, such as the birds bring to their young, but on dangerous nationalistic fantasies. Then, added to this comparison, is an invocation to the future, that a 'sweetness'—a positive and joyful mode of living—may come to inhabit the emptiness which he and his friends will leave, or which they represent. (Both the 'emptiness' and the nest, of course, are suggestive in various different ways: the nest is pictured as empty, but they are also empty men; the discarded nest suggests Ireland but also the poet's ageing body.) There follows in Section VII one of those apocalyptic visions of which Yeats was master even in the days of *The Wind Among the Reeds*. He pictures, in a feverish and dissolving phantasmagoria, dangerous and threatening forms of that self-delight and that passion and violence he has meditated on before, and following on their heels a third spectre, more threatening than either, that of an inhuman predatory indifference. The poet, appalled by these visions, renounces all yearnings for a life of action and influence over men (the kind of life that counts as 'success' among ordinary people) and resolves to content himself with his solitary and occult studies.

This edifying and, as you might say, Wordsworthian conclusion, with its resigned acceptance of a life dealing only in 'abstract' things (the fate envisaged so bitterly in Section I of 'The Tower') strikes me as just a shade forced, as if the poet did not quite mean it even at the time of writing. ('Abstract' is always a very pejorative word for Yeats, who, like 'modernist' poets in general, regarded abstraction as the arch-enemy of poetry.) However, we realise, this is very much an interim stage of feeling, which will be superseded, 'dialectically', by others, and moreover we must not confuse the imaginary poet who is speaking with Yeats himself.

THE STRUCTURE OF *THE TOWER*

In discussing the first three poems in *The Tower* I have been stressing the 'argument', the train of thought connecting the stanzas or sections of the poems. I would like now, for the rest of the volume, to examine the train of thought connecting one poem with another. This seems to me fairly obvious with the first three poems, or at least its main direction, and I hope our discussion has helped to bring it out. So let us start at the point we have now reached, that is to say with the fourth poem in the volume, 'Nineteen Hundred and Nineteen'. And at this point, if you have not done so before, you should give a first reading to the whole volume.

'Nineteen Hundred and Nineteen' is a poem rather similar to 'Meditations in Time of Civil War' in its general shape and

Les Licornes by Gustave Moreau. This painting was a source for the last section of 'Meditations in Time of Civil War'. (Musée Gustav Moreau. Photo Bulloz)

particularly so in that it ends, as does 'Meditations', with a phantasmagoric vision of a world returning to chaos and the rule of evil. But one asks oneself why this poem, which deals with the year 1919 and the 'Troubles' (the guerilla fighting between the British and the newly formed IRA), should come after not before a poem dealing with the Civil War, that is to say a period four years later. Part of the answer, I suggest, is that 'Nineteen Hundred and Nineteen' is not so similar to 'Meditations' as it appears. It is not what I have called a 'dialectical' poem like the preceding one, setting up statements and counter-statements and resolving these in a third statement, which then becomes the starting point of a further dialectical argument, and so on. Yeats's mind is still working dialectically, but now on a larger scale, arranging whole poems and groups of poems in this dialectical way. The poem 'Nineteen Hundred and Nineteen', complex though it is, adds up to a single statement; the counter-statement and the resolution are spread over a number of succeeding poems.

'Nineteen Hundred and Nineteen' is, I would say, essentially a political poem. It says that the political assumptions and hopes of the poet and his friends have been proved false by the brutal and chaotic course of events in Europe since 1914 and in Ireland since 1916. The assumptions of his youth were those of the Gladstone era: gradually, it seemed, civilization, tolerance and large mindedness were beginning to prevail in the world and drum-and-trumpet militarism was becoming an anachronism. This hope is now discredited; there is no progress in history, only an endless cyclical recurrence of old errors. Hence the only fit response to history and politics is pessimism and mockery, a mockery as deep as one can make it. And as for the poet himself, as a private person, he must be content after all not to leave a legacy. Those proud claims on posterity asserted in 'The Tower' and 'Meditations in Time of Civil War' were vain. The best he can hope for is, in the brief interval of his life, to have constructed a self-image by means of his art. Indeed, he begins to feel the pull of death and a kind of savage pleasure at the thought of leaving his work half-done.

The next poem, 'The Wheel', explicitly deals with this yearning for death, picturing man's perpetual restlessness as being, at bottom, a longing for death. 'The New Faces' (addressed, we may guess, to Lady Gregory, now an old woman near death) depicts the poet as instinctively taking sides with the dead against the living. These are the natural emotions of an ageing man, acknowledging that in the natural course of things his own 'day' is over, but, equally naturally, feeling resentment and pessimism.

Then we have 'A Prayer for my Son' which expresses, what is equally natural to an ageing man, a protectiveness and care for his child, his physical posterity. This is a simple counter-statement to the preceding poems. He has written, from various angles and in various tones, about old age and the inheritance he might or might not leave;

the subject which logically follows is posterity, which is to say birth.

A lot more is involved in this transition, however. In 'A Prayer for my Son' the poet prays to Christ to protect his son, and thereby launches himself on a whole new set of thoughts. For Christ's own birth was no simple domestic event, nor an unmixed Christmas-card-like happiness. It put an end to the whole pagan world. It could, from one point of view, be regarded as an event of terror, destroying the civilized Greek tradition of reason and tolerance (as, on a smaller scale, the events after 1916 seemed to destroy or discredit nineteenth-century liberalism) and ushered in fanaticism, persecution and the Dark Ages. 'A Prayer for my Son', which so beautifully evokes, like some early Renaissance painting, the human tenderness of the Holy Family in their flight from Herod, is followed by 'Two Songs from a Play', in which the Virgin appears as a bloodstained executioner of the pagan gods. The juxtaposition could not be more dramatic.

'Fragments' provides another example of 'terrible' births: the poet pictures the Industrial Revolution (symbolized by the spinning jenny) as being born from the ribs of John Locke,* the prophet of Augustan rationalism, just as Eve† was born from Adam's side—and like that earlier event, ushering in a new era at vast and painful cost (another loss of Eden). 'Leda and the Swan' provides a third instance (foreshadowed in the lines about Troy in 'Two Songs from a Play'): Zeus, disguised as a swan, begets Helen upon Leda, thereby engendering the whole cycle of the Trojan wars. (We can aptly call this engendering a 'birth'.)

There are many interlocking ways in which we can interpret this seeing of birth as, potentially, a painful and terrible event, and one of them is personal to Yeats. The whole volume, *The Tower*, is about a transition in the poet's life, the deeply painful transition we call, banally, 'facing up to the facts of age and death', and he draws an implicit parallel between giving way to a new generation—which, though painful, is the poet's own fate and the fate of every man—and the giving way of one historic era to another, also a painful and perhaps terrible process. Such a comparison, by itself, would seem far-fetched and overweening; but we remember that, as compensation for quitting the country of the young, the poet has promised himself a kind of new birth and the acquiring of some kind of 'supernatural' powers, and with this in mind the idea acquires much human meaning. For the births of Christ and of Helen of Troy, as he depicts them—being likewise conjunctions of the supernatural with the natural—are seen as painful and terrible. And this leads to a very

---

* John Locke (1632–1704), educationalist, Whig political writer and founder of the analytical tradition in English philosophy. Yeats was not the first to trace a connection between the Industrial Revolution and Locke's views.

† Note the neatness and wittiness of Yeats's symbol: Eve also span, if we are to believe the rhyme 'When Adam delved and Eve span, where was then the gentleman?'

simple question: is giving up one's natural life for a supernatural one a desirable thing? Would it be worth it?

The poet asks this very question in the poem 'Among School Children', and I will jump over 'On a Picture of a Black Centaur by Edmund Dulac' for a moment to pursue the point. In 'Among School Children' the poet asks (in stanza V), would a young mother, were she able to see her son as he would be at sixty, now 'a comfortable kind of old scarecrow', think it worth all the agony of child-bearing? From this very simple question, he is led on to the thought that a mother, in adoring her young child, is an image-worshipper, just as much as a nun adoring a crucifix; and adoring images, or, what is similar, sacrificing one's life to some dream or ideal—and here we remember Yeats's notion of the artist's life as a continual, gruelling effort to create an ideal anti-self—is a heart-breaking business. The image-worshipper is in conflict with himself, he is breaking himself into two; whereas happiness, if happiness were possible, would lie in being *one*, not divided against oneself, living from one's own self-delight.

I will go back now to 'On a Picture of a Black Centaur by Edmund Dulac'. It is a puzzling poem, or I should say a puzzle-poem, a poem which has come to Yeats in a dream or perhaps in a spiritualistic seance, and we should not try to explicate its symbolism too literally; at any rate I have not managed to myself and am not too clear what those 'horrible green parrots' stand for. But the general drift is clear: in the past the poet has cultivated the wrong kind of magical knowledge and powers:

> I, being driven half insane
> Because of some green wing, gathered old mummy wheat
> In the mad abstract dark and ground it grain by grain
> And after baked it slowly in an oven;

Now, however, he has found the right, healthy kind, an ancient wisdom that has matured like wine.

This is another, and the last, turning-point in the volume; for all the remaining poems, including 'Among School Children', are meant to exemplify this healthy and cheerful wisdom. From this point on the poet has succeeded—as was the desperate endeavour of the old man in 'Sailing to Byzantium—in freeing himself from the envy of the young and rage at his own lost youth. The next poem, 'Colonus' Praise' (a chorus from Yeats's translation of Sophocles's tragedy *Oedipus at Colonus*), confirms this. Like the old King Oedipus, blind, blasted by fate and outlawed from his own kingdom, the poet is welcomed into a new and hospitable country. This, it seems, *is* a country for old men.

What I would draw your attention to is the way that Yeats, in adapting Sophocles, contrives to give him a note of genial and pastoral jollity:

> Immortal ladies tread the ground
> Dizzy with harmonious sound,
> Semele's lad a gay companion.

('Semele's lad' is his jocular name for the great Dionysus, god of wine.)

'Wisdom' elaborates the witty and light-hearted notion that Christianity did not properly begin till the Middle Ages, when the messy reality had been tidied up and replaced by a charming, idealized religious art. Christ's infancy, when he became 'wild' in the normal, carefree way of the human child, effaced the horror of his birth from his Mother's mind, after which Christianity became a cheerful affair.

'The Fool by the Roadside' gives a ballad-like gaiety to Yeats's cyclical theory of history. And in 'Owen Aherne and his Dancers' Yeats writes, very autobiographically, and again in a song-like or ballad-like manner, about his abortive proposal to Iseult Gonne, one of the bitter experiences which have driven his heart 'mad' with chagrin; the poem resignedly acknowledges that 'wildness', the natural joyous wildness of youth, must not be caged. In 'A Man Young and Old' he then gives a ballad-like version of a life such as his own has been, ending with another chorus from *Oedipus at Colonus*— an inspired transition from the popular to the solemn, for which he has prepared by that jovial 'pastoral' note I mentioned in the earlier chorus. 'The Three Monuments', referring to Dublin statues of Nelson, Parnell and O'Connell, mocks blithely at the stuffy orthodoxy which pretends that their secret was 'purity', whereas it was wildness.

Then, finally, in 'All Souls' Night', the poet once again conjures up ghosts (as did the old man in 'Sailing to Byzantium' and the poet in 'The Tower'), and offers them some of his wholesome wine to taste— that wine we first heard of in 'On a Picture of a Black Centaur by Edmund Dulac'. His tone is now full of tingling but serene excitement, that of man in harmony with himself. Previously, the ghosts have been invoked to give aid to or answer questions; now it is the other way round and the poet has a 'truth' to offer to the ghosts.

We need not feel cheated that the poet does not actually tell us what this 'truth' is. Any truth that Yeats has to tell is embodied in the poems of *The Tower* and the way that they are joined together. He found a memorable expression of this in the last years of his life, when he said: 'It seems to me that I have found what I wanted. When I try to put all into a phrase, I say, "Man can embody truth but he cannot know it".' (Letter to Lady Elizabeth Pelham, 4 January 1939.) Admittedly, Yeats being the man he was, if you had asked him for the truth about the universe he would probably have told you it, or at least given you a résumé of *A Vision*. ('All Souls' Night' appears as the epilogue to *A Vision*.) However, his answer would probably have disappointed you. And so far as 'All Souls' Night' is concerned, the

Maud Gonne MacBride. (National Library of Ireland)

poet's having a marvellous 'truth' to deliver (should he find a drinking-companion worthy to hear it) is a poetic fiction. It is a fiction necessary to complete the imagined fictional progress from exile to sage, from desperation to reconcilement and transcendence, and is shot through with as many ironies and reservations as any of Yeats's poetic fictions.

'AMONG SCHOOL CHILDREN'

I want, finally, to look again at 'Among School Children'. It is generally felt to be one of Yeats's finest poems, so I make no apology for dwelling on it further. To get to know this poem really well is as sure a way as you can find towards getting to the heart of Yeats. It is not, in general, a difficult poem—or only 'difficult' in the sense that *King Lear* is difficult: that is to say more rich, more achieved, more inexhaustible than most works of art. A good deal has been written about it, though; and I have listed one or two essays, which give a slightly different account from mine, in the Further Reading list at the end.

The thing I would stress myself is how many varied thoughts and feelings have been set in order in the poem, how much territory one finds that, by the end of it, one has covered, by following its devious but unbroken argument. Another point: one sometimes gets the impression from reading about Yeats that he produced poems in a void and simply by continual meditation on his own private symbols and obsessions; indeed, sometimes he himself wished it could be that way. I do not think good poetry can ever be produced like that; and certainly the present poem was not created in a vacuum, it sprang absolutely naturally out of an incident in the everyday world. The sixty-year-old Yeats (for once, perhaps, there is no harm in saying 'Yeats', not 'the poet') is visiting a convent school: a famous literary figure, performing the kind of slightly boring duty that is expected of public men. Everyone, including himself, is on their best behaviour, and the nun in charge explains the school's teaching methods—which as Yeats's tone conveys, strike him as conventional, tame and irrelevant to all the vital concerns of life. It is a situation of wry comedy: he himself feels tame and commonplace and just a shade ridiculous. The girls look at him with 'momentary wonder', but this mangy old lion can mean nothing to them.

The spectacle of these girls puts him in mind of Maud Gonne and stories she once told him by the fireside about her own childhood and its pains, and of how their intimate talk made them feel like twin souls. (The reference to Plato refers to the notion of his *Symposium* that the sexes are the severed halves of a sphere, continually longing to be reunited.) He asks himself if she ever resembled the girls in the schoolroom; for, though she had qualities—aristocratic breeding and

Senator W. B. Yeats c. 1936. (BBC Hulton Picture Library)

goddess-like grace and beauty—that they will never possess (we must swallow Yeats's snobbery as best we can), she too must have had an 'ugly duckling' stage. The thought revives all his passion for her, driving his heart 'wild': in his mind's eye he pictures her simultaneously as an awkward child and as she is now, still beautiful but ravaged by time: old as he is old. He too was handsome and had 'pretty plumage' once, he tells himself. 'Pretty plumage' is literally very apt, as well as suiting his metaphor, for Yeats as a young man had a bird-like crest of long hair; but what is more essential is how the phrase sustains the tone, that tone of genial and wry irony, which has predominated so far. He stops himself immediately from self-pity ('enough of that')—here is an example of that 'talking in verse' of which Yeats is by now such a master—and directs his thought away to the general human condition. (This is a familiar movement of thought in Yeats; you will remember something like it in 'The Cold Heaven'.)

❧   I find that phrase 'the uncertainty of his setting forth' (in stanza V) intensely suggestive. What are some of the meanings packed up in the phrase, would you say?

Discussion
I take it: the mother's uncertainties about what will happen to the boy when he leaves home, and the boy's own uncertainties; but also the uncertainties that surround the whole of human existence and the 'journeying' of the soul. ❧

The next stanza may strike you as difficult and hold you up for a bit. However, the allusions to Plato, Aristotle and Pythagoras are fundamentally fairly simple (though very brilliant). The poet is saying, I think, that all these philosophers despised nature and the visible world. Plato thought of the visible world as merely a thin and unreal covering upon the true reality, which consisted in certain 'ideas' or archetypes laid up in heaven. Aristotle was 'solider' (i.e., he believed somewhat more in the reality of the physical world) for did he not when he was tutor to Alexander the Great, use the strap on his royal pupil's bottom? (Which must at least have convinced his pupil that the physical world was real!) All the same, Aristotle was arrogant in thinking a mere philosopher had much to teach a man who represented all the world's power and glory. Then there was a third philosopher, Pythagoras, who located reality in music and mathematics. Reality, as pictured by all these philosophers, was no more than a stiff scarecrow dressed up in old clothes, a scarecrow like the poet's own ageing self—fit to make schoolgirls laugh.

The poem now makes a startling leap of thought to what seems to be a quite new subject, and at the same time its tone also shifts, to a grand and impersonal poignancy and gravity. By pausing here and pondering why it is not, after all, a break in the train of thought but a necessary continuation of it, one begins to get a grasp of the scope of the poem as a whole. I have already roughly paraphrased the thought in the stanza itself on p. 64 so what I would add here is merely how extraordinarily fine those lines 'Both nuns and mothers worship images . . .' seem to me. In an essay, 'The Study of Poetry' (1888), the critic Matthew Arnold collected certain great lines and passages in which he found what he called 'The accent of high seriousness, born of absolute sincerity', and he suggested using them as 'touchstones' to help us 'keep clear and sound our judgements about poetry, to save us from fallacious estimates of it'. Arnold's language is old-fashioned and Victorian-sounding, but I think there is something to be said for his 'touchstone' theory; and I would elect these lines of Yeats's as one of my touchstones for genuineness in poetry. There is a kind of impersonality in them, as though this was a thought that lay about for anyone to have, had he the wit and feeling to do so; and—though this is not necessarily a criterion of greatness—the thought would survive translation into another language.

We come to the last stanza. The poet has mocked the philosophers for despising nature, which is greater than they are. He has voiced fellow-feeling for all those for whom beauty is something which has to be paid for in agony and heartbreak. He now, in a tone in which bitterness, pity and questioning intellect are still present (the stanza ends with two questions), but which is predominantly joyful, unenvious and affirmative, says that true happiness in life, could it be found (and perhaps it can), would exist where the natural life was enjoyed, and beauty achieved, without self-division and conflict. Notice the expressively ambiguous syntax in 'Labour is blossoming or dancing where . . .', which evades paraphrase, though the ambiguity derives from the fact that 'blossoming' may be a noun but could also be a participle: it does *not* mean the same as 'Labour becomes something joyful like blossoming or dancing when . . . etc'. The fact that one cannot paraphrase these two lines, or work out the exact grammatical relations of the words in them, is important and suggests the same notion as Yeats goes on to express when asking 'O chestnut-tree, great rooted blossomer/Are you the leaf, the blossom or the bole?'. And what underlies this unanswerable question, and partly explains its joyful tone, is the unspoken thought that in a poem like 'Among School Children' the poet has achieved—momentarily, and no doubt through painful toil and plenty of midnight oil—the kind of natural, flexible, integrated and self-sufficient beauty (so unlike a rigid scarecrow dressed up in makeshift clothes) that is the finest flowering of human life. He has written a poem that exists, and is beautiful, in its own right and can *not* be paraphrased. One cannot, ultimately, say of it that its content or message is such-and-such and that the poet has expressed this in such-and-such a manner. In a poem like this, meaning and form are indistinguishable, and to ask which is which would be like asking whether a tree was its leaf, its blossom or its bole.

Afterword

Here are some suggestions for further work on Yeats.

MAKING YOUR OWN ANTHOLOGY

You should, above all, go on dipping into *Collected Poems*, sampling all his various collections, and if any poems catch your fancy especially (or alternatively if they irritate you) pondering the reasons why. It might help if you did this not quite randomly but following up some theme. You might, for instance, make a collection of poems of Yeats's addressed to, or concerned with, *his friends*. They are a very characteristic part of his work and include some magnificent poems. One or two which spring to mind are: 'Friends' (p. 139), 'In Memory of Major Robert Gregory' (p. 148), 'In Memory of Eva Gore-Booth and Con Markiewicz' (p. 263), 'Beautiful Lofty Things' (p. 348), 'The Municipal Gallery Revisited' (p. 368); there are many more. Or you could collect poems sparked off by contemporary events: for instance 'Upon a House Shaken by the Land Agitation' (p. 106), 'To a Wealthy Man, etc.' (p. 119), 'On Those that Hated *The Playboy of the Western World*' (p. 124), or the little group of political poems you will find in the middle of *Michael Robartes and the Dancer*. Or again—this is a more general theme—one could say that it was a characteristic of Yeats, as revealed in his poems, that, having pursued transcendence of the human state (by religious or mystical or magical means) there is a recoil—he comes down to earth again; he reminds himself how fond he is, when all is said and done, of ordinary foolish everyday life. It is the theme of an early poem 'To the Rose upon the Rood of Time' (p. 35)— a very equivocal poem, by the way—and recurs again in late poems. like 'A Dialogue of Self and Soul' (p. 265) and 'Vacillation' (p. 282). I may not have found the best way of describing it, but whatever it is, it is something important to Yeats. By collecting further examples of it, you might see further into its significance.

72

STUDYING PARTICULAR BOOKS

Another thing you might do is to choose one other of Yeats's collections of verse and try to trace out its design—its overall structure or 'plot'—in the way that I attempted with *The Tower*. One good choice for this might be *Michael Robartes and the Dancer* (1921): it is relatively short, carefully organized and a good example of middle-period Yeats. Another, and more ambitious, choice would be *The Winding Stair* (1933). This would have the special interest that it is very closely connected with *The Tower*, being, as I have said earlier, regarded by Yeats as in some sense an 'answer' to the earlier volume. (Whether or not you choose this collection, you should make a point of comparing the poem 'Byzantium' in it with 'Sailing to Byzantium' in *The Tower*; the two poems extend each other's meaning.)

YEATS AS DRAMATIST

Yeats wrote plays throughout his career and was also a leading figure in the foundation of the famous Abbey Theatre in Dublin. As a dramatist (unlike many of those he sponsored at the Abbey Theatre) he was in strong revolt against the current 'realist' trend in drama. In his early period he wrote numerous plays, more or less supernatural in flavour, on themes from ancient Irish mythology. Of these *The Countess Cathleen* (staged in 1899) is a good example and was often performed. During World War I he wrote several verse-dramas in the style of the Japanese *Noh* play. Of these *At the Hawk's Well* (1916) is an undoubted masterpiece, which should not be missed. The powerful one-act drama *Purgatory* (1938), composed in his later years, is also widely regarded as one of the finest achievements of twentieth-century verse drama. There is a performance of this play on the Audio-cassette which accompanies this pack.

YEATS AS PROSE WRITER

I would urge you to sample Yeats as a prose writer. There is, of course, one very characteristic example of his prose printed here as Appendix III: 'A General Introduction for my Work'. Apart from this, if you can get hold of it, I would particularly recommend his *Autobiographies*. In every way, personally, historically and intellectually, it is a most absorbing work, which can't help but enlarge your idea of this extraordinary man.

YEATS IN HIS TIMES

In many of the poems you have been studying, it is evident that Yeats is both responding and contributing to the Irish struggle for national independence. To learn more about his ambition to become the poet of a united Irish consciousness, and his relationship with the events of his time, you might first look at a biography of Yeats, then at one or other of the many studies of the Irish cultural and national revival, as well as general works on Irish history. A few of the better known works are listed under Further Reading, and many of these will have bibliographies which will enable you to go further.

If you are interested in Yeats's political views, a good place to begin is Conor Cruise O'Brien's famous essay, 'Passion and Cunning: An Essay on the Politics of W. B. Yeats', in Jeffares and Cross (1965) and then Elizabeth Cullingford's book on *Yeats, Ireland and Fascism*, 1981.

Appendix I.
Notes on some allusions
in The Tower

I have explained certain of Yeats's allusions in *The Tower* in the course of my discussion of the volume, and various others are explained by Yeats himself in his notes at the end of *Collected Poems*. A few more notes may be helpful, however and further information can be found in Jeffares (1968).

'THE TOWER'

Ben Bulben   A mountain near Yeats's grandfather's home in Co. Sligo.
Plotinus   Neoplatonic philosopher and mystic (*c*. 207–70 AD).
the Great Memory   A concept somewhat akin to Jung's Collective Unconscious.
Burke   Edmund Burke (1729–1797), British statesman and political philosopher, of Irish origin. In his early days he was a leading opponent of 'tyranny', or at least pretensions to autocratic government, on the part of George III.
Grattan   Henry Grattan (1746–1820), Irish statesman and patriot. The short-lived independent parliament in Ireland of 1782–1801 was known as 'Grattan's Parliament'.

'MEDITATIONS IN TIME OF CIVIL WAR'

daemonic rage   A *daemon* or *daimon* is a lesser kind of divinity or tutelary spirit, and 'rage' is used here in the sense of 'state of inspiration'.
Sato   During Yeats's American tour in 1920 a Japanese, Junzo Sato, presented him with a sword which had been in Sato's family for five hundred years.
Primum Mobile   According to the ancient Ptolemaic theory of the Universe, the Earth was surrounded by nine revolving concentric crystalline spheres, carrying the stars and planets, and a tenth, the Primum Mobile, which gave motion to all the rest. Yeats is using the Ptolemaic system as a metaphor for his own theory of 'gyres' or

recurrent patterns in history. He likewise, having in the previous stanza established owls as a symbol of desolation, makes metaphoric use of their wheeling flight.

'NINETEEN HUNDRED AND NINETEEN'

pitches   the literal meaning must be 'hurls' or 'tosses'. In Yeats's own theory of the Universe human events and changes are related to the phases of the Moon, which can thus be said to 'pitch' earthly things about (as a ship on a high sea pitches passengers and cargo about).

An ancient image made of olive wood   This was a cult statue of the goddess Athene reputed to have fallen from heaven and greatly prized by the Athenians. From the account of it in Pausanias it appears to have stood in the Erechteum. Tertullian called it a shapeless log.

Phidias   No work from the hand of the famous Athenian sculptor Phidias has survived, though he designed the Parthenon sculptures.

Loie Fuller   An American dancer who performed at the Folies Bergère in Paris, surrounding herself with a whirl of iridescent draperies. Mallarmé wrote an essay on her.

Platonic Year   The Great Year of Plato, the period at the end of which all the planets would return to their original positions. Its length was estimated variously, though 36,000 calendar years is the most commonly agreed figure.

Some Platonist etc.   An allusion to the doctrine of reincarnation.

Herodias' daughters   See Yeats's note to 'The Hosting of the Sidhe' on p. 524 of *Collected Poems*.

Lady Kyteler   Robert Artisson (see Yeats's note) was the 'incubus' of a certain Dame Alice Kyteler.

'TWO SONGS FROM A PLAY'

The play in question is Yeats's *The Resurrection* (1927), which turns on the notion that Christ's coming brought to an end a two-thousand-year cycle of history. At the end of the play a rationalistic Greek, who believes that the resurrected Christ is only a phantom, places his hand on Christ's side and discovers, to his terror, that the heart is beating. He declares: 'O Athens, Alexandria, Rome, something has come to destroy you. The heart of a phantom is beating. Man has begun to die. Your words are clear at last, O Heraclitus, God and man die each other's life, live each other's death.'

The two songs are sung by a musician at, respectively, the opening and the close of the play.

holy Dionysus   A passage in Sir James Frazer's *The Golden Bough* throws light on the parallel which Yeats is drawing between the resurrection myth associated with the Greek Dionysus and the resurrection of Christ. I will quote the account given in Jeffares (1968):

> Dionysus, child of a mortal Persephone, and an immortal, Zeus, was torn to pieces by the Titans. Athene . . . snatched the heart from his body, brought it on her hand to Zeus, who killed the Titans, swallowed the heart, and begat Dionysus again, upon another mortal, Semele.

Magnus Annus   Latin for 'The Great Year' (see earlier note).
Another Troy etc.   Yeats is drawing on a famous prophetic passage in Virgil's fourth Eclogue:

> Yet shall some few traces of olden sin lurk behind, to call men to essay the sea in ships, to gird towns with walls, and to cleave the earth with furrows. A second Tiphys shall then arise, and a second Argo to carry chosen heroes; a second warfare, too, shall there be, and again shall a great Achilles be sent to Troy.

Babylonian starlight   See the next note.

'LEDA AND THE SWAN'

The poem appears at the beginning of Book V of *A Vision* ('Dove or Swan'), in which Yeats outlines his theory of cyclical patterns in history. He writes there:

> I imagine the annunciation that founded Greece as made to Leda, remembering that they showed in a Spartan temple, strung up to the roof as a holy relic, an unhatched egg of hers; and that from one of her eggs came Love and from the other War. But all things are from antithesis, and when in my ignorance I try to imagine what older civilisation that annunication rejected I can but see bird and woman blotting out some corner of the Babylonian mathematical starlight.

His remarks about 'Babylonian mathematical starlight' means, clearly, that the only impression he can form of the civilization which preceded the Greek one (and was brought to an end by it) is that it was a civilization governed by Babylonian astrologers. This gives us a certain help in explaining 'Babylonian starlight' in 'Two Songs from a Play'; presumably the 'fabulous, formless darkness' he speaks of there must refer to early Greek civilizations—(i.e., he is saying, 'just as early Greek civilization [foretold by the astrologers of Babylon, which preceded it] began as something formless and irrational, so did the Christian era which succeeded it').
the broken wall etc.   i.e. of Troy.
Agamemnon dead   Agamemnon was murdered on his return home from Troy by his wife Clytemnestra and her lover Aegisthus.

'ON A PICTURE OF A BLACK CENTAUR BY EDMUND DULAC'

Edmund Dulac French Painter and book-illustrator (1882–1953) with whom Yeats was friendly.

mummy wheat Wheat found in the wrappings of ancient Egyptian mummies. Reputedly, it will still germinate; but perhaps Yeats is saying that this is just what it would not do.

seven Ephesian topers The 'Seven Sleepers of Ephesus', Christian youths who took refuge in a cave from the persecutions of the Emperor Decius and slept for two hundred years. Calling them 'topers' (i.e., drinkers or drunkards), is Yeats's own embroidery on the legend.

Saturnian The reign of Saturn, early god-king of Italy, became known as the Golden Age. By 'Saturnian' Yeats perhaps means 'as tranquil as the Golden Age'.

'AMONG SCHOOL CHILDREN'

Quattrocento finger i.e. the finger of a fifteenth-century sculptor such as Donatello.

golden-thighed A picturesque detail about the philosopher Pythagoras which Yeats found in Thomas Taylor's translation of Iamblichus's *Life of Pythagoras*.

'COLONUS' PRAISE'

Sophocles' *Oedipus at Colonus* was a work of his old age dealing with events later than those referred to in *Oedipus Rex*. In it the ill-fated King Oedipus, banished from Thebes, comes to Colonus, near Athens, with his daughter Antigone and finds sanctuary there.

olive-tree There was a sacred olive tree in the Erechteum at Athens, bestowed by the city's patron the goddess Athene, which miraculously grew out of the bare stone.

the Great Mother etc. Demeter, earth mother, goddess of the harvest, mourning her daughter Persephone, who, while gathering flowers, was carried off to the underworld by Pluto. (Demeter wandered the earth in search of her, and at her prayer, Zeus allowed Persephone to return to earth for six months of each year.)

Cephisus A river in Attica.

Poseidon gave it bit and oar Poseidon (identified by the Romans with their water god) bestowed on mankind the use of the horse and of ships.

'WISDOM'

Noah's freshet   A whimsical phrase for the Flood. (A 'freshet' is a small stream.)

'OWEN AHERNE AND HIS DANCERS'

Owen Aherne is a character in the title story of Yeats's *The Tables of the Law* (1897).
Norman upland   Yeats made his proposal to Iseult Gonne when they were staying in Normandy in the summer of 1917.

'A MAN YOUNG AND OLD'

'The Death of the Hare'   Yeats once, when asked, said that this poem 'means that the lover may while loving feel sympathy with his beloved's dread of captivity' (Hone, 1962, p. 441).
great Hector   The Trojan leader, slain by the Greek Achilles, and hence, in a certain sense, one of Helen's victims.

'THE THREE MONUMENTS'

The poem was originally written to ridicule the Irish Senate's reluctance to pass a Divorce Bill.

'ALL SOULS' NIGHT'

All Souls' Day (1 November) is a festival on which prayers are offered for the souls of the faithful departed. Yeats, in his character of one with occult knowledge to reveal, summons up the ghosts of old associates of his in the Order of the Golden Dawn (see pp. 7–8).
Christ Church   An Oxford college whose chapel is the cathedral of Oxford.
Horton   W. T. Horton, author of *A Book of Images* (1898), to which Yeats wrote a preface.
Florence Emery   An actress, née Florence Farr. She was a close friend of Yeats's and collaborated with him in experiments in the speaking of verse to music.
MacGregor   MacGregor Mathers, chief organizer and leading spirit of the Order of the Golden Dawn in its early days but subsequently expelled, partly through Yeats's own efforts.

Appendix II.
Yeats's A Vision

I have mentioned that Yeats constructed an elaborate occult system or philosophy, publishing it as *A Vision* in 1925 and re-issuing it in drastically revised form in 1937. To have done so was evidently a great satisfaction to Yeats himself and was a means of assuring himself that the insights in his poems had philosophical coherence. What use the common reader can make of his 'system' is less certain and has been much debated. Many critics, despite exasperation, do find *A Vision* a great help in understanding Yeats's poems, and it would be absurd to deny that it can be some help. Nevertheless, my own feeling is that things are mainly the other way round, and that the poems help one to understand *A Vision* much more than *A Vision* helps one to understand the poems. Yeats is less interesting when he is systematizing than when he is writing poems. Thus my own advice would be: read·*A Vision* (and its rum and very entertaining assemblage of prefaces) if you feel curious; but if you do not manage to do so, do not fear that you have neglected the 'key' to his poetry.

Yeats claimed to have received the metaphysical system set forth in *A Vision* by dictation from certain 'Instructors', situated—as spiritualists would say—'on the other side'. The system was quite different in character from the magical and cabbalistic one he had earlier studied in the Order of the Golden Dawn, and it was some time, so he said, before he properly understood it, especially its geometrical part. There was, to begin with, a difficulty about technical terms. It so happened that his Instructors had been reading his book *Per Amica Silentia Lunae* (1918), and they suggested adopting the term 'antithetical' used by him in this book. He in turn contributed the term 'tincture', which he had found in the works of the German mystic Jacob Boehme. The Instructors dictated through his wife, first of all by means of automatic writing and later by automatic speech, in both cases at such a speed that Yeats could take notes. All was not easy, however, for there was trouble with 'Frustrators' who interposed fraudulent messages, and when this was discovered to have happened Yeats had to scrap many days' notes. The whole process of transmission took several years. The result, in the form given to it by Yeats in *A Vision* (the first version of which was published in 1925) was a mixture of sacred book and philosophical treatise. Some parts claim to be 'ins-

pired' and to reveal truths—for instance those about the afterlife—
that were to be taken on trust. Other parts, we may assume, were
meant to represent Yeats's own contribution. This must be so, because
the theory of life propounded in the book is very close, in some
respects, to ideas Yeats had expressed in prose and verse long before
the Instructors entered his life.

The central principle of the system is the notion that all human
existence follows the pattern described by the Greek philosopher
Heraclitus in the words 'Dying each other's life, living each other's
death', or by Empedocles when he spoke of existence as ruled by the
twin principles of Discord and Concord. ('When Discord has fallen
into the lowest depths of the vortex Concord has reached the centre.')
This pattern, so Yeats's Instructors told him, could be expressed
geometrically as a double cone or vortex (see overleaf). Each cone
represents the bounds of a spiral or 'gyre', which is made by the
unwinding of thread from a bobbin (or 'perne'); so the cone can also
be depicted as shown overleaf (below).

Yeats explains:

> If we think of the vortex attributed to Discord as formed by circles
> diminishing until they are nothing, and of the opposing sphere
> attributed to Concord as forming from itself an opposing vortex, the
> apex of each vortex in the middle of the other's base, we have the
> fundamental symbol of my instructors.
>
> If I call the unshaded cone 'Discord' and the other 'Concord' and
> think of each as the bounds of a gyre, I see that the gyre of 'Concord'
> diminishes as that of 'Discord' increases, and can imagine after that
> the gyre of 'Concord' increasing while that of 'Discord' diminishes;
> and so on, one gyre within the other always.
>
> (*A Vision*, p. 68)

According to this view, human life can be seen as composed of
intersecting states struggling one against the other, and, particularly,
as a seesaw between two opposed principles: the principle of
objectivity (named by Yeats or his Instructors the 'primary principle')
that is to say the knowing and realising of the world as it exists, and
the principle of subjectivity (named the 'antithetical' principle),
which is concerned with realising an inner world of desire and
imagination (the principle of the mask). These principles Yeats found
it convenient to call 'tinctures'. Thus, reverting to the diagram overleaf, the unshaded cone or triangle represents the 'antithetical tincture'
and the shaded one the 'primary tincture'. As one 'tincture' opens, the
other 'tincture' closes.

The scheme is very general in its application: it can be used to
describe or explain the differences in human temperament, or it can
be used to explain the pattern of history. Thinking for a moment of
human temperament: a typical example of the dominance of the

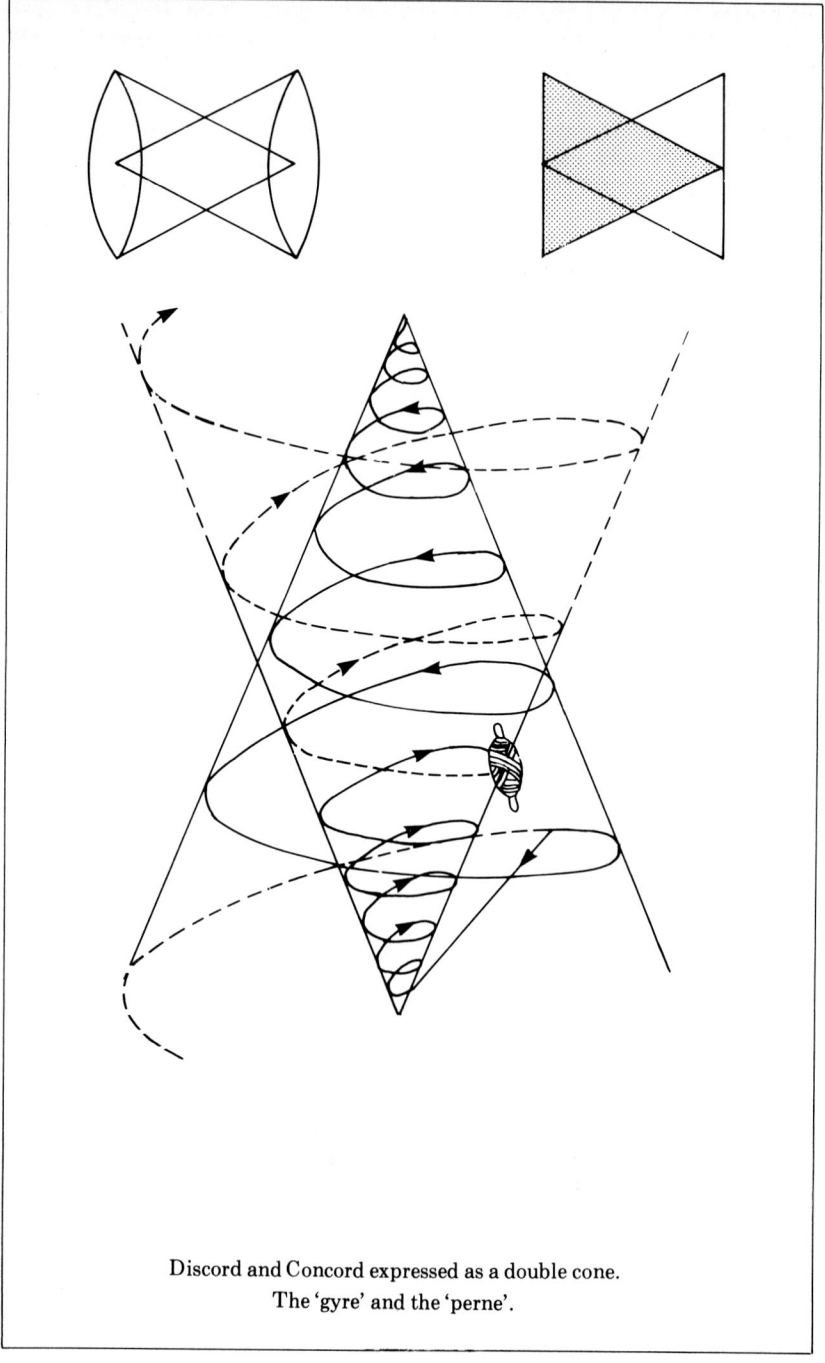

Discord and Concord expressed as a double cone.
The 'gyre' and the 'perne'.

'primary' tincture would be men and women like Queen Victoria, Galsworthy or Lady Gregory, who, says Yeats, think of life in terms of a cut-and-dried code of conduct received from outside themselves. Typical of the dominance of the antithetical tincture, on the other hand, would be the artist, like Yeats himself, a man who invents his own ideals and whose life is a continual struggle to realise a self which is the opposite of all he is in daily life.

A system of human character-types can be drawn up, according to the relative dominance of the antithetical or the primary. However, it must now be explained that there are really not two things but four things involved: the antithetical principle or tincture is to be thought of as a combination of *Will* and the *Mask* (the will, and the object or ideal which it pursues), and the primary tincture as a combination of *Creative Mind* and *Body of Fate* (thought and knowledge, the Knower and the Known). Will and Mask and Creative Mind and Body of Fate are known as the *Four Faculties* (these Faculties are what men have made for themselves through many incarnations). Going back to our diagrams: as Will (and its mask) approaches the utmost expansion of the cone, thought becomes almost completely dominated by will, but on reaching the extreme expansion of its cone will weakens ('as though satiated'), and the reverse process begins.

As I have said, a system of human character-types can be charted according to their position in this seesawing process; and Yeats draws up just such a chart: he entitles it 'The Twenty-eight Incarnations',

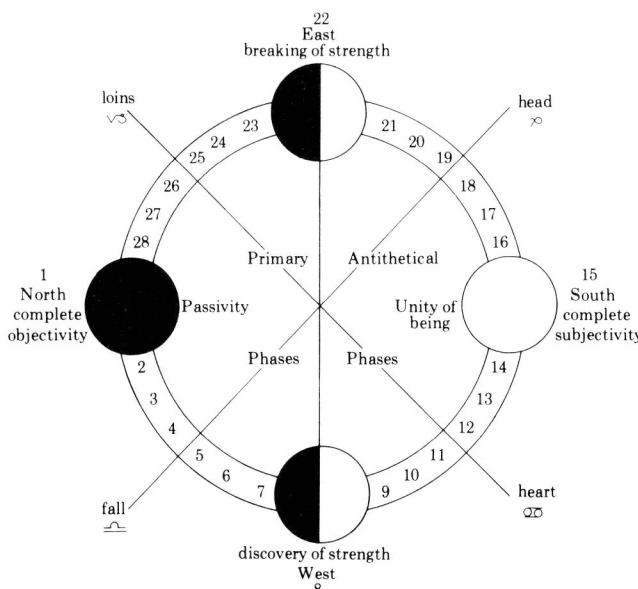

The twenty-eight incarnations.

and it occupies a considerable part of his book. Why it should be twenty-eight has now to be explained: it is because his Instructors told him to connect his character-types with the twenty-eight phases of the Moon.

And to complicate things further, it emerges that the whole process, which we have hitherto considered as a matter of interlocking 'gyres' or cones, can also be thought of as a *wheel*. Yeats's diagram of the *Great Wheel*, the numbers along the rim showing the Moon's twenty-eight phases, is shown above.

You will see that the points of the compass are also involved, but I haven't the space to go into that here.

What the symbol of the wheel emphasizes is that Yeats's system is not merely a static affair but involves motion. That is to say, in his view, any particular phase in the relations of Will and Mask to Creative Mind and Body of Fate tends to produce the next phase. This is easily understood when applied to history. Yeats sees history as a cyclical movement, each stage or phase in a civilization automatically producing a particular successor (according to a pattern similar to that of his twenty-eight character-types), until all the phases have been run through and the process starts again. (He pictures civilizations as being a more-and-more strenuous effort at self-control—in which they would resemble a human being striving to perfect his mask—and then this self-control as finally breaking down in violence and disorder; whereupon a new era is born).

Yeats's wheel and his gyres have a complicated relation to each other. Thus, he explains: 'This wheel is every completed movement of thought or life, twenty-eight incarnations, a single incarnation, a single judgement or act of thought.' (*A Vision*, p. 81). Again, his twenty-eight character-types (or 'phases' or 'incarnations') have a number of complicated mathematical inter-relations. Each 'phase' turns out to have its opposite, or mirror image, at the appropriate number up or down the scale; and again, each 'triad', or group of three successive phases, has a similar structure. Thanks to these mathematics Yeats claimed, optimistically, that he now possessed 'a classification of every possible movement of thought and of life'.

We still have not done, for it turns out that the afterlife has its own system, in which the *Four Faculties* are replaced by *Four Principles* (*Husk, Passionate Body, Spirit* and *Celestial Body*) which, as Yeats explains, are 'the Faculties transferred, as it were, from a concave to a convex mirror, or vice versa'. Also, the period of the afterlife, that is to say the period between death and re-birth, is divided into six stages, namely: *Vision of the Blood Kindred*, the *Meditation* (or the *Dreaming Back*), the *Shiftings*, the *Marriage* (or *Beatitude*), the *Purification*, and the *Foreknowledge*. These successive states are related to astrology and the Zodiac.

Most readers of *A Vision* tear their hair with exasperation at moments. What is unsatisfactory in it, in my own view, is, in the first place, one's doubts about Yeats's relationship with his Instructors. Of course, it may be that there *are* 'Instructors' on 'the other side' and that they read the latest books (of course with miraculous celerity) and undertake to give lessons to deserving pupils. On the other hand, if there are not, as I am inclined to think, then Yeats has enacted an extraordinary comedy of self-deception—and this is a fact one cannot ignore. (There seems to be no other alternative, for I think we can dismiss the possibility that he or his wife consciously practised deception.)

Then, to my mind, a metaphysical system, if it is to be any good, ought to be worked out exhaustively, even if this means drily and dustily, and Yeats's is not: one moment he is systematic, full of tables and diagrams, the next he is poetic, suggestive and elusive. Book III, 'The Soul in Judgment', in which we are told about the adventures of the soul between death and birth, is particularly baffling. There is genius in those marvellous names, the *Dreaming Back*, the *Shiftings* and so on, but one has no idea whether to treat the book as revelation or as something Yeats has made up. Its connection with the general system is vague, moreover. Yeats's remark about concave and convex mirrors is magnificent but conversation-stopping.

His dealings with history are relatively sketchy too, or seem so if one compares his 'Dove or Swan' section with other such cyclical views of history, like Oswald Spengler's *The Decline of the West* (1918–23)— a book which he read—or with Arnold Toynbee's *A Study of History* (1934–1954). As Yeats freely admits, his knowledge of history was scrappy, and, plainly, a century or two either way made little difference in his eyes. He knew exactly what pattern he was looking for in history and somewhat capriciously cast about for evidence which fitted it. I mean by this no reflection on his historical intuitions, which again were those of genius; only on his pretensions to documentation.

By far the most thoroughly worked-out section is Book I, Part III, 'The Twenty-eight Incarnations', and here admiration creeps in. His account of Phase Twenty-four, for instance—the one typified by Queen Victoria, Galsworthy and Lady Gregory—is a most profound and acute analysis of a certain attitude to life. (It strikes me, in passing, how similar in some ways Yeats's view of life was to Tolstoy's: in *Anna Karenina* we find the same fundamental distinction drawn between those, like Vronsky and the Oblonskys, who think of life in terms of a code accepted from outside, and those, like Levin, who, through struggle, create their own ideals for themselves. Levin is a perfect example of antithetical man.)

Another passage, Yeats's description of Phase Fifteen, is even more impressive and illuminating. This is clearly Yeats's favourite among the phases, and his account of it is, among other things, a description of the condition of mind which produces great art. In ways which it would take too long to go into here, you will see that it has close relevance to 'Among School Children'. I will end by quoting the whole passage, thus giving you a taste of this bizarre system in action.

PHASE FIFTEEN
Will.
Mask (from Phase 1).
Creative Mind (from Phase 15)   No description except that this is
Body of Fate (from Phase 1).   a phase of complete beauty.

Body of Fate and *Mask* are now identical; and *Will* and *Creative Mind* identical; or rather the *Creative Mind* is dissolved in the *Will* and the *Body of Fate* in the *Mask*. Thought and will are indistinguishable, effort and attainment are indistinguishable; and this is the consummation of a slow process; nothing is apparent but dreaming *Will* and the Image that it dreams. Since Phase 12 all images, and cadences of the mind, have been satisfying to that mind just in so far as they have expressed this converging of will and thought, effort and attainment. The words 'musical', 'sensuous', are but descriptions of that converging process. Thought has been pursued, not as a means but as an end—the poem, the painting, the reverie has been sufficient of itself. It is not possible, however, to separate in the understanding this running into one of *Will* and *Creative Mind* from the running into one of *Mask* and *Body of Fate*. Without *Mask* and *Body of Fate* the *Will* would have nothing to desire, the *Creative mind* nothing to apprehend. Since Phase 12 the *Creative mind* has been so interfused by the *antithetical tincture* that it has more and more confined its contemplation of actual things to those that resemble images of the mind desired by the *Will*. The being has selected, moulded and remoulded, narrowed its circle of living, been more and more the artist, grown more and more 'distinguished' in all preference. Now contemplation and desire, united into one, inhabit a world where every beloved image has bodily form, and every bodily form is loved. This love knows nothing of desire, for desire implies effort, and though there is still separation from the loved object, love accepts the separation as necessary to its own existence. *Fate* is known for the boundary that gives our *Destiny* its form, and—as we can desire nothing outside that form—as an expression of our freedom. Chance and Choice have become interchangeable without losing their identity. As all effort has ceased, all thought has become image, because no thought could exist if it were not carried towards its own extinction, amid fear or in contemplation; and every image is separate from every other, for if image were linked to image, the soul would awake from its immovable trance. All that the being has experienced as thought is visible to its eyes as a whole, and in this way it perceives, not as they are to others, but according to its own perception, all orders of existence. Its own body possesses the greatest possible beauty, being indeed that body which the soul will permanently inhabit, when all its phases have been repeated according to the number allotted: that which we call the clarified or Celestial Body. Where the being has lived out of phase, seeking to live through *antithetical* phases as though they had been *primary*, there is now terror of solitude, its forced, painful and slow acceptance, and a life haunted by terrible dreams. Even for the most perfect, there is a time of pain, a passage through a vision, where evil reveals itself in its final meaning. In this passage Christ, it is said, mourned over the length of time and the unworthiness of man's lot to man, whereas his forerunner mourned and his successor will mourn over the shortness of time and the unworthiness of man to his lot; but this cannot yet be understood.

Appendix III:
Yeats's 'A general introduction for my work'*

1 THE FIRST PRINCIPLE

A poet writes always of his personal life, in his finest work out of its tragedy, whatever it be, remorse, lost love, or mere loneliness; he never speaks directly as to someone at the breakfast table, there is always a phantasmagoria. Dante and Milton had mythologies, Shakespeare the characters of English history or of traditional romance; even when the poet seems most himself, when he is Raleigh and gives potentates the lie, or Shelley 'a nerve o'er which do creep the else unfelt oppressions of this earth', or Byron when 'the soul wears out the breast' as 'the sword outwears its sheath', he is never the bundle of accident and incoherence that sits down to breakfast; he has been reborn as an idea, something intended, complete. A novelist might describe his accidence, his incoherence, he must not; he is more type than man, more passion than type. He is Lear, Romeo, Oedipus, Tiresias; he has stepped out of a play, and even the woman he loves is Rosalind, Cleopatra, never The Dark Lady. He is part of his own phantasmagoria and we adore him because nature has grown intelligible, and by so doing a part of our creative power. 'When mind is lost in the light of the Self,' says the Prashna Upanishad,† 'it dreams no more; still in the body it is lost in happiness.' 'A wise man seeks in Self,' says the Chandogya Upanishad, 'those that are alive and those that are dead and gets what the world cannot give.' The world knows nothing because it has made nothing, we know everything because we have made everything.

2 SUBJECT-MATTER

It was through the old Fenian leader John O'Leary I found my theme.§ His long imprisonment, his longer banishment, his mag-

* Written [in 1937] for a complete edition of Yeats's works which was never produced. First published as W. B. Yeats (1961) 'A general introduction for my work', in *Essays and Introductions*, Macmillan, Basingstoke, pp. 509–526.
† [The *Upanishads* form part of the ancient sacred books of the Hindus, known as the *Vedas*.]
§ [See 'September 1913' in *Collected Poems*, p. 120.]

nificent head, his scholarship, his pride, his integrity, all that
aristocratic dream nourished amid little shops and little farms, had
drawn around him a group of young men; I was but eighteen or
nineteen and had already, under the influence of *The Faerie Queene*
and *The Sad Shepherd* [pastoral play by Ben Jonson, published
1641], written a pastoral play, and under that of Shelley's
Prometheus Unbound two plays, one staged somewhere in the
Caucasus, the other in a crater of the moon; and I knew myself to be
vague and incoherent. He gave me the poems of Thomas Davis [Irish
poet and journalist (1814–1845)], said they were not good poetry but
had changed his life when a young man, spoke of other poets
associated with Davis and *The Nation* newspaper, probably lent me
their books. I saw even more clearly than O'Leary that they were not
good poetry. I read nothing but romantic literature; hated that dry
eighteenth-century rhetoric; but they had one quality I admired and
admire: they were not separated individual men; they spoke or tried
to speak out of a people to a people; behind them stretched the
generations. I knew, though but now and then as young men know
things, that I must turn from that modern literature Jonathan Swift
compared to the web a spider draws out of its bowels; I hated and still
hate with an ever growing hatred the literature of the point of view. I
wanted, if my ignorance permitted, to get back to Homer, to those
that fed at his table. I wanted to cry as all men cried, to laugh as all
men laughed, and the Young Ireland poets when not writing mere
politics had the same want, but they did not know that the common
and its befitting language is the research of a lifetime and when found
may lack popular recognition. Then somebody, not O'Leary, told me
of Standish O'Grady [historian and novelist (1846–1928)] and his
interpretation of Irish legends. O'Leary had sent me to O'Curry, but
his unarranged and uninterpreted history defeated my boyish
indolence.

A generation before *The Nation* newspaper was founded the Royal
Irish Academy had begun the study of ancient Irish literature. That
study was as much a gift from the Protestant aristocracy which had
created the Parliament as *The Nation* and its school, though Davis
and Mitchell were Prostestants, was a gift from the Catholic middle
classes who were to create the Irish Free State. The Academy
persuaded the English Government to finance an ordnance survey on
a large scale; scholars, including that great scholar O'Donovan, were
sent from village to village recording names and their legends.
Perhaps it was the last moment when such work could be well done,
the memory of the people was still intact, the collectors themselves
had perhaps heard or seen the banshee; the Royal Irish Academy and
its public with equal enthusiasm welcomed Pagan and Christian;
thought the Round Tower a commemoration of Persian fire-
worship. There was little orthodoxy to take alarm; the Catholics were
crushed and cowed; an honoured great-uncle of mine—his portrait by
some forgotten master hangs upon my bedroom wall—a Church of
Ireland rector, would upon occasion boast that you could not ask a
question he could not answer with a perfectly appropriate blasphemy

or indecency. When several counties had been surveyed but nothing published, the Government, afraid of rousing dangerous patriotic emotion, withdrew support; large manuscript volumes remain containing much picturesque correspondence between scholars.

When modern Irish literature began, O'Grady's influence predominated. He could delight us with an extravagance we were too critical to share; a day will come, he said, when Slieve-na-mon will be more famous than Olympus; yet he was no Nationalist as we understood the word, but in rebellion, as he was fond of explaining, against the House of Commons, not against the King. His cousin, that great scholar Hayes O'Grady, would not join our non-political Irish Literary Society because he considered it a Fenian body, but boasted that although he had lived in England for forty years he had never made an English friend. He worked at the British Museum compiling their Gaelic catalogue and translating our heroic tales in an eighteenth-century frenzy; his heroine 'fractured her heart', his hero 'ascended to the apex of the eminence' and there 'vibrated his javelin', and afterwards took ship upon 'colossal ocean's superficies'. Both O'Gradys considered themselves as representing the old Irish land-owning aristocracy; both probably, Standish O'Grady certainly, thought that England, because decadent and democratic, had betrayed their order. It was another member of that order, Lady Gregory, who was to do for the heroic legends in *Gods and Fighting Men* and in *Cuchulain of Muirthemne* what Lady Charlotte Guest's *Mabinogion* had done with less beauty and style for those of Wales. Standish O'Grady had much modern sentiment, his style, like that of John Mitchel forty years before, shaped by Carlyle; she formed her style upon the Anglo-Irish dialect of her neighbourhood, an old vivid speech with a partly Tudor vocabularly, an syntax partly moulded by men who still thought in Gaelic.

I had heard in Sligo cottages or from pilots at Rosses Point endless stories of apparitions, whether of the recent dead or of the people of history and legend, of that Queen Maeve whose reputed cairn stands on the mountain over the bay. Then at the British Museum I read stories Irish writers of the 'forties and 'fifties had written of such apparitions, but they enraged me more than pleased because they turned the country visions into a joke. But when I went from cottage to cottage with Lady Gregory and watched her hand recording that great collection she has called *Visions and Beliefs* I escaped disfiguring humour.

Behind all Irish history hangs a great tapestry, even Christianity had to accept it and be itself pictured there. Nobody looking at its dim folds can say where Christianity begins and Druidism ends; 'There is one perfect among the birds, one perfect among the fish, and one among men that is perfect.' I can only explain by that suggestion of recent scholars—Professor Burkitt of Cambridge commended it to my attention—that St. Patrick came to Ireland not in the fifth century but towards the end of the second. The great controversies had not begun; Easter was still the first full moon after the Equinox. Upon that day the world had been created, the Ark rested upon

Ararat, Moses led the Israelites out of Egypt; the umbilical cord
which united Christianity to the ancient world had not yet been cut,
Christ was still the half-brother of Dionysus. A man just tonsured by
the Druids could learn from the nearest Christian neighbour to sign
himself with the Cross without sense of incongruity, nor would his
children acquire that sense. The organized clans weakened Church
organization, they could accept the monk but not the bishop.

A modern man, *The Golden Bough** and *Human Personality*† in
his head, finds much that is congenial in St. Patrick's Creed as re-
corded in his Confessions, and nothing to reject except the word 'soon'
in the statement that Christ will soon judge the quick and the dead.
He can repeat it, believe it even, without a thought of the historic
Christ, or ancient Judea, or of anything subject to historical conjecture
and shifting evidence; I repeat it and think of 'the Self' in the
Upanishads. Into this tradition, oral and written, went in later years
fragments of Neo-Platonism, cabbalistic words—I have heard the
words 'tetragrammaton agla' in Doneraile—the floating debris of
mediaeval thought, but nothing that did not please the solitary
mind. Even the religious equivalent for Baroque and Rococo could
not come to us as thought, perhaps because Gaelic is incapable of
abstraction. It came as cruelty. That tapestry filled the scene at the
birth of modern Irish literature, it is there in the Synge of *The Well of
the Saints*, in James Stephens, and in Lady Gregory throughout, in
all of George Russell that did not come from the Upanishads, and in
all but my later poetry.

Sometimes I am told in commendation, if the newspaper is Irish,
in condemnation if English, that my movement perished under the
firing squads of 1916; sometimes that those firing squads made our
realistic movement possible. If that statement is true, and it is only
so in part, for romance was everywhere receding, it is because in the
imagination of Pearse [Sinn Fein leader (1879–1916)] and his fellow
soldiers the Sacrifice of the Mass had found the Red Branch in the
tapestry; they went out to die calling upon Cuchulain: §

> Fall, Hercules, from Heaven in tempests hurled
> To cleanse the beastly stable of this world.

In one sense the poets of 1916 were not of what the newspapers call
my school. The Gaelic League, made timid by a modern populariza-
tion of Catholicism sprung from the aspidistra and not from the root
of Jesse, dreaded intellectual daring and stuck to dictionary and
grammar. Pearse and MacDonagh and others among the executed

---

*[Famous work on primitive beliefs by Sir James Frazer, first published in 1890.]
†[*Human Personality and its Survival of Bodily Death* by Frederick W. H. Myers
(1903).]
§[Cuchulain was a famous hero in the cycle of Irish sagas concerning the 'Red Branch
Knights'. Yeats's meaning seems to be that, in the imagination of Pearse and his fellows
in the Easter Rebellion of 1916, Catholicism joined with heroic and Pagan Irish
tradition.]

men would have done, or attempted, in Gaelic what we did or attempted in English.

Our mythology, our legends, differ from those of other European countries because down to the end of the seventeenth century they had the attention, perhaps the unquestioned belief, of peasant and noble alike; Homer belongs to sedentary men, even today our ancient queens, our mediaeval soldiers and lovers, can make a pedlar shudder. I can put my own thought, despair perhaps from the study of present circumstance in the light of ancient philosophy, into the mouth of rambling poets of the seventeenth century, or even of some imagined ballad singer of today, and the deeper my thought the more credible, the more peasant-like, are ballad singer and rambling poet. Some modern poets contend that jazz and music-hall songs are the folk art of our time, that we should mould our art upon them; we Irish poets, modern men also, reject every folk art that does not go back to Olympus. Give me time and a little youth and I will prove that even 'Johnny, I hardly knew ye' goes back.

Mr. Arnold Toynbee in an annex to the second volume of *The Study of History* describes the birth and decay of what he calls the Far Western Christian culture; it lost at the Synod of Whitby its chance of mastering Europe, suffered final ecclesiastical defeat in the twelfth century with 'the thoroughgoing incorporation of the Irish Christendom into the Roman Church. In the political and literary spheres' it lasted unbroken till the seventeenth century. He then insists that if 'Jewish Zionism and Irish Nationalism succeed in achieving their aim, then Jewry and Irishry will each fit into its own tiny niche . . . among sixty or seventy national communities', find life somewhat easier, but cease to be 'the relic of an independent society . . . the romance of Ancient Ireland has at last come to an end. . . . Modern Ireland has made up her mind, in our generation, to find her level as a willing inmate in our workaday Western world.'

If Irish literature goes on as my generation planned it, it may do something to keep the 'Irishry' living, nor will the work of the realists hinder, nor the figures they imagine, nor those described in memoirs of the revolution. These last especially, like certain great political predecessors, Parnell, Swift, Lord Edward [Fitzgerald (1763–1798) Irish patriot and rebel], have stepped back into the tapestry. It may be indeed that certain characteristics of the 'Irishry' must grow in importance. When Lady Gregory asked me to annotate her *Visions and Beliefs* I began, that I might understand what she had taken down in Galway, an investigation of contemporary spiritualism. For several years I frequented those mediums who in various poor parts of London instruct artisans or their wives for a few pence upon their relations to their dead, to their employers, and to their children; then I compared what she had heard in Galway, or I in London, with the visions of Swedenborg, and, after my inadequate notes had been published, with Indian belief. If Lady Gregory had not said when we passed an old man in the woods, 'That man may know the secret of the ages,' I might never have talked with Shri Purohit Swāmi* nor made him translate his Master's travels in Tibet, nor helped him translate the Upanishads. I think I now know why the gamekeeper at Coole heard the footsteps of a deer on the edge of the lake where no deer had passed for a hundred years, and why a certain cracked old priest said that nobody had been to hell or heaven in his time, meaning thereby that the Rath had got them all; that the dead stayed where they had lived, or near it, sought no abstract region of blessing or punishment but retreated, as it were, into the hidden character of their neighbourhood. I am convinced that in two or three generations it will become generally known that the mechanical theory has no reality, that the natural and supernatural are knit together, that to escape a dangerous fanaticism we must study a new science; at that moment Europeans may find something attractive in a Christ posed against a background not of Judaism but of Druidism, not shut off in dead history, but flowing, concrete, phenomenal.

I was born into this faith, have lived in it, and shall die in it; my Christ, a legitimate deduction from the Creed of St. Patrick as I think, is that Unity of Being Dante compared to a perfectly proportioned human body, Blake's 'Imagination', what the Upanishads have named 'Self': nor is this unity distant and therefore intellectually understandable, but imminent, differing from man to man and age to age, taking upon itself pain and ugliness, 'eye of newt, and toe of frog'.

Subconscious preoccupation with this theme brought me *A Vision* [Yeats's mystical and philosophical treatise, published 1925], its harsh geometry an incomplete interpretation. The 'Irishry' have preserved their ancient 'deposit' through wars which, during the sixteenth and seventeenth centuries, became wars of extermination; no people, Lecky said at the opening of his *Ireland in the Eighteenth Century*, have undergone greater persecution, nor did that persecution altogether cease up to our own day. No people hate as we do in whom that past is always alive, there are moments when hatred poisons my life and I accuse myself of effeminacy because I have not given it adequate expression. It is not enough to have put it into the mouth of a rambling peasant poet. Then I remind myself that though mine is the first English marriage I know of in the direct line, all my family names are English, and that I owe my soul to Shakespeare to Spenser and to Blake, perhaps to William Morris, and to the English language in which I think, speak, and write, that everything I love has come to me through English; my hatred tortures me with love, my love with hate. I am like the Tibetan monk who dreams at his initiation that he is eaten by a wild beast and learns on waking that he himself is eater and eaten. This is Irish hatred and solitude, the hatred of human life that made Swift write *Gulliver* and the epitaph

* [Yeats wrote an Introduction to Shri Purohit Swāmi's translation of Bhagwan Shri Hamsa's *The Holy Mountain*.]

upon his tomb,* that can still make us wag between extremes and doubt our sanity.

Again and again I am asked why I do not write in Gaelic. Some four or five years ago I was invited to dinner by a London society and found myself among London journalists, Indian students, and foreign political refugees. An Indian paper says it was a dinner in my honour; I hope not; I have forgotten, though I have a clear memory of my own angry mind. I should have spoken as men are expected to speak at public dinners; I should have paid and been paid conventional compliments; then they would speak of the refugees; from that on all would be lively and topical, foreign tyranny would be arraigned, England seem even to those confused Indians the protector of liberty; I grew angrier and angrier; Wordsworth, that typical Englishman, had published his famous sonnet to François Dominique Toussaint, † a Santo Domingo Negro:

> There's not a breathing of the common wind
> That will forget thee

in the year when Emmet conspired and died, and he remembered that rebellion as little as the half hanging and the pitch cap that preceded it by half a dozen years. That there might be no topical speeches I denounced the oppression of the people of India; being a man of letters, not a politician, I told how they had been forced to learn everything, even their own Sanskrit, through the vehicle of English till the first discoverer of wisdom had become bywords for vague abstract facility. I begged the Indian writers present to remember that no man can think or write with music and vigour except in his mother tongue. I turned a friendly audience hostile, yet when I think of that scene I am unrepentant and angry.

I could no more have written in Gaelic than can those Indians write in English; Gaelic is my national language, but it is not my mother tongue.

3 STYLE AND ATTITUDE

Style is almost unconscious. I know what I have tried to do, little what I have done. Contemporary lyric poems, even those that moved me—'The Stream's Secret', 'Dolores' [Swinburne, from *Poems and Ballads,* First Series]—seemed too long, but an Irish preference for a swift current might be mere indolence, yet Burns may have felt the same when he read Thomson and Cowper. The English mind is meditative, rich, deliberate; it may remember the Thames valley. I planned to write short lyrics or poetic drama where every speech

---

* [It reads: *Ubi saeva indignatio ulterius cor lacerare nequit*—'Where fierce indignation can no longer tear his heart'.]
† [Toussaint L'Ouverture, a negro, led a successful slave-revolt in the French colony of San Domingo (Haiti) in 1791.]

would be short and concentrated, knit by dramatic tension, and I did so with more confidence because young English poets were at that time writing out of emotion at the moment of crisis, though their old slow-moving meditation returned almost at once. Then, and in this English poetry has followed my lead, I tried to make the language of poetry coincide with that of passionate, normal speech. I wanted to write in whatever language comes most naturally when we soliloquize, as I do all day long, upon the events of our own lives or of any life where we can see ourselves for the moment. I sometimes compare myself with the mad old slum women I hear denouncing and remembering; 'How dare you,' I heard one say of some imaginary suitor, 'and you without health or a home!' If I spoke my thoughts aloud they might be as angry and as wild. It was a long time before I had made a language to my liking; I began to make it when I discovered some twenty years ago that I must seek, not as Wordsworth thought, words in common use, but a powerful and passionate syntax, and a complete coincidence between period and stanza. Because I need a passionate syntax for passionate subject-matter I compel myself to accept those traditional metres that have developed with the language. Ezra Pound, [W. J.] Turner [1889–1946], Lawrence wrote admirable free verse, I could not. I would lose myself, become joyless like those mad old women. The translators of the Bible, Sir Thomas Browne, certain translators from the Greek when translators still bothered about rhythm, created a form midway between prose and verse that seems natural to impersonal meditation; but all that is personal soon rots; it must be packed in ice or salt. Once when I was in delirium from pneumonia I dictated a letter to George Moore telling him to eat salt because it was a symbol of eternity; the delirium passed, I had no memory of that letter, but I must have meant what I now mean. If I wrote of personal love or sorrow in free verse, or in any rhythm that left it unchanged, amid all its accidence, I would be full of self-contempt because of my egotism and indiscretion, and foresee the boredom of my reader. I must choose a traditional stanza, even what I alter must seem traditional. I commit my emotion to shepherds, herdsmen, camel-drivers, learned men, Milton's or Shelley's Platonist, that tower Palmer* drew. Talk to me of originality and I will turn on you with rage. I am a crowd, I am a lonely man, I am nothing. Ancient salt is best packing. The heroes of Shakespeare convey to us through their looks, or through the metaphorical patterns of their speech, the sudden enlargement of their vision, their ecstasy at the approach of death: 'She should have died hereafter' [Macbeth, on the death of Lady Macbeth], 'Of many thousand kisses, the poor last' [Antony to Cleopatra], 'Absent thee from felicity awhile' [Hamlet]. They have become God or Mother Goddess, the pelican, 'My baby at my breast,' but all must be cold; no actress has ever sobbed when she played Cleopatra, even the shallow brain of a producer has never thought of such a thing. The

* [The tower with its lighted window depicted by Samuel Palmer (1805–1851) in his illustrations to Milton's 'Il Penseroso' exercised a great hold on Yeats's imagination.]

supernatural is present, cold winds blow across our hands, upon our faces, the thermometer falls, and because of that cold we are hated by journalists and groundlings. There may be in this or that detail painful tragedy, but in the whole work none. I have heard Lady Gregory say, rejecting some play in the modern manner sent to the Abbey Theatre, 'Tragedy must be a joy to the man who dies.' Nor is it any different with lyrics, songs, narrative poems; neither scholars nor the populace have sung or read anything generation after generation because of its pain. The maid of honour whose tragedy they sing must be lifted out of history with timeless pattern, she is one of the four Maries, the rhythm is old and familiar, imagination must dance, must be carried beyond feeling into the aboriginal ice. Is ice the correct word? I once boasted, copying the phrase from a letter of my father's, that I would write a poem 'cold and passionate as the dawn'.

When I wrote in blank verse I was dissatisfied; my vaguely med-iaeval *Countess Cathleen* fitted the measure, but our Heroic Age went better, or so I fancied, in the ballad metre of *The Green Helmet.* There was something in what I felt about Deirdre, about Cuchulain, that rejected the Renaissance and its characteristic metres, and this was a principal reason why I created in dance plays the form that varies blank verse with lyric metres. When I speak blank verse and analyse my feelings, I stand at a moment of history when instinct, its traditional songs and dances, its general agreement, is of the past. I have been cast up out of the whale's belly though I still remember the sound and sway that came from beyond its ribs, and, like the Queen in Paul Fort's ballad, I smell of the fish of the sea. The contrapuntal structure of the verse, to employ a term adopted by Robert Bridges, combines the past and present. If I repeat the first line of *Paradise Lost* so as to emphasize its five feet I am among the folk singers—'Of mán's fírst disobédience ánd the frúit,' but speak it as I should I cross it with another emphasis, that of passionate prose—'Of mán's fírst disobédience and the frúit,' or 'Of mán's fírst dísobedience and the frúit'; the folk song is still there, but a ghostly voice, an unvariable possibility, an unconscious norm. What moves me and my hearer is a vivid speech that has no laws except that it must not exorcize the ghostly voice. I am awake and asleep, at my moment of revelation, self-possessed in self-surrender; there is no rhyme, no echo of the beaten drum, the dancing foot, that would overset my balance. When I was a boy I wrote a poem upon dancing that had one good line: 'They snatch with their hands at the sleep of the skies.' If I sat down and thought for a year I would discover that but for certain syllabic limitations, a rejection or acceptance of certain elisions, I must wake or sleep.

The Countess Cathleen could speak a blank verse which I had loosened, almost put out of joint, for her need, because I thought of her as mediaeval and thereby connected her with the general European movement. For Deirdre and Cuchulain and all the other figures of Irish legend are still in the whale's belly.

4 WHITHER?

The young English poets reject dream and personal emotion; they have thought out opinions that join them to this or that political party; they employ an intricate psychology, action in character, not as in the ballads character in action, and all consider that they have a right to the same close attention that men pay to the mathematician and the metaphysician. One of the more distinguished has just explained that man has hitherto slept but must now awake. They are determined to express the factory, the metropolis, that they may be modern. Young men teaching school in some picturesque cathedral town, or settled for life in Capri or in Sicily, defend their type of metaphor by saying that it comes naturally to a man who travels to his work by Tube. I am indebted to a man of this school who went through my work at my request,* crossing out all conventional metaphors, but they seem to me to have rejected also those dream associations which were the whole art of Mallarmé. He had topped a previous wave. As they express not what the Upanishads call 'that ancient Self' but individual intellect, they have the right to choose the man in the Tube because of his objective importance. They attempt to kill the whale, push the Renaissance higher yet, out-think Leonardo; their verse kills the folk ghost and yet would remain verse. I am joined to the 'Irishry' and I expect a counter-Renaissance. No doubt it is part of the game to push that Renaissance; I make no complaint; I am accustomed to the geometrical arrangement of history in *A Vision*, but I go deeper than 'custom' for my convictions. When I stand upon O'Connell Bridge† in the half-light and notice that discordant architecture, all those electric signs, where modern heterogeneity has taken physical form, a vague hatred comes up out of my own dark and I am certain that wherever in Europe there are minds strong enough to lead others the same vague hatred rises; in four or five or in less generations this hatred will have issued in violence and imposed some kind of rule of kindred. I cannot know the nature of that rule, for its opposite fills the light; all I can do to bring it nearer is to intensify my hatred. I am no Nationalist, except in Ireland for passing reasons; State and Nation are the work of intellect, and when you consider what comes before and after them they are, as Victor Hugo said of something or other, not worth the blade of grass God gives for the nest of the linnet.

---

* [Presumably Ezra Pound.]
† [The bridge crossing the River Liffey at the end of O'Connell Street, in the centre of Dublin.]

References and Further Reading

TEXTS

The standard texts of Yeats's work are as follows:

Collected Poems (1950), Macmillan, Basingstoke (2nd edn).
Collected Plays (1952), Macmillan, Basingstoke.
Autobiographies (1965), Macmillan, Basingstoke (2nd edn).
Essays and Introduction (1961), Macmillan, Basingstoke.
Explorations (1962), Macmillan, Basingstoke.
Mythologies (1962), Macmillan, Basingstoke.
A Vision (1965), Macmillan, Basingstoke (rev edn).
Wade, A. (ed.) (1954), *The Letters of W. B. Yeats*, Hart Davis, London.
Pearse, D. R. (ed.) (1961), *The Senate Speeches of W. B. Yeats*, Faber and Faber, London.
Most of these are now available in paperback editions.

BIOGRAPHY

Hone, J. (1962), *W. B. Yeats, 1865–1939*, Macmillan, Basingstoke (rev. edn).
Tuohy, F. (1976), *Yeats*, Macmillan, Basingstoke. This book has many fascinating illustrations.
There is also important biographical material in the books by Ellman and Jeffares listed below.

READER'S GUIDES

Jeffares, A. N. (1968), *A Commentary on the Collected Poems of W. B. Yeats*, Macmillan, Basingstoke.
Malins, E. (1974) *A Preface to Yeats*, Longman, Harlow. Contains much useful reference material.
Unterecker, J. (1959), *A Reader's Guide to W. B. Yeats*, Thames and Hudson, London. Perhaps somewhat less satisfactory, being a mixture of simple exposition and of critical interpretation.

CRITICISM

Bloom, H. (1970), *Yeats*, Oxford University Press.
Brooks, C. (1968), 'Yeats's great rooted blossomer', in his *The Well Wrought Urn*, Methuen, London. A discussion of 'Among School Children'.
Eliot, T. S. (1957), *On Poets and Poetry*, Faber and Faber, London.
Ellmann, R. (1948), *Yeats: the Man and the Masks*, Macmillan, Basingstoke.
Ellmann, R. (1954), *The Identity of Yeats*, Oxford University Press.
Henn, T. R. (1950), *The Lonely Tower: Studies in the Poetry of W. B. Yeats*, Methuen, London.
Hough, G. (1949), *The Last Romantics*, Duckworth, London. Good on Yeats's relation to the nineteenth century.
Jeffares, A. N. (1949), *W. B. Yeats, Man and Poet*, Routledge and Kegan Paul, London.
Jeffares, A. N. and Cross, K. G. W. (eds) (1965), *In Excited Reverie*, Macmillan, Basingstoke.
Kermode, F. (1957), *Romantic Image*, Routledge and Kegan Paul, London. Good on the influence of Symboliste theories upon Yeats's later poetry and on 'Among School Children'.
Leavis, F. R. (1969), 'Yeats, the problem and the challenge', in *Lectures in America* (with Leavis, Q. D.), Chatto, London.
MacNeice, L. (1941), *The Poetry of W. B. Yeats*, Oxford University Press.
Stead, G. K. (1964), *The New Poetic*, Hutchinson, London.
Melchiori, G. (1961), *The Whole Mystery of Art*, Macmillan, Basingstoke. Valuable on the sources for the 'Byzantium' poems.
Rudd, M. E. (1953), *The Divided Image: Study of William Blake and W. B. Yeats*, Routledge and Kegan Paul, London.
Unterecker, J. (ed.) (1963), *Yeats: A Collection of Critical Essays*, Prentice-Hall, New York.
Wilson, F. A. C. (1958), *Yeats and Tradition*, Macmillan, Basingstoke.
Yeats's revisions can be studied in Allt, P. and Alspach, R. K. (eds) (1957), *The Variorum Edition of the Poems of W. B. Yeats*, Macmillan, Basingstoke, which gives a complete listing of them, and in Stallworthy, J. (1963), *Between the Lines*, Oxford University Press, which discusses them.

GENERAL

Beckett, J. C. (1952), *A Short History of Ireland*, Hutchinson, London.
Beckett, J. C. (1976), *The Anglo-Irish Tradition*, Faber and Faber, London.

Cullingford, E. (1981), *Yeats, Ireland and Fascism*, Macmillan, Basingstoke.

Jeffares, A. N. (1982), *Anglo-Irish Literature*, Macmillan, Basingstoke.

Lyons, F. S. L. (1973), *Ireland since the Famine* (rev. edn), Fontana, London.

Lyons, F. S. L. (1978), *Culture and Anarchy in Ireland*, Clarendon Press, Oxford.

Marcus, P. L. (1970), *Yeats and the Beginning of the Irish Renaissance*, Cornell University Press, New York.

Glossary

ALLITERATION   Repetition of the same initial sound. For instance as in C. Day Lewis's line: 'As one who wanders into old workings'.

ASSONANCE   The chiming of similar vowel sounds. For instance, in Yeats's 'The Lake Isle of Innisfree', the chiming of the vowel sounds indicated by accents:

> I will arise and go now, and go to Innisfrée,
> And a small cabin build there, of cláy and wattles máde:
> Nine béan-rows will I have there, a hive for the honey-bée,
> And live alone in the bee-loud glade.

BALLAD-STANZA   A common verse form for a ballad is a quatrain of alternate four-foot and three-foot iambic lines, the second and fourth lines rhyming. For instance:

> Clerk Saunders and May Margaret
>   Walk'd o'er yon garden green;
> And deep and heavy was the love
>   That fell thir twa between.

There are, however, many variants of the ballad-stanza.

BLANK VERSE   Verse in unrhymed iambic pentameters. For example:

> This whole day have I followed in the rocks,
> And you have changed and flowed from shape to shape,
> First as a raven on whose ancient wings
> Scarcely a feather lingered, then you seemed
> A weasel moving on from stone to stone,
> And now at last you wear a human shape,
> A thin grey man half lost in gathering night.
>
> (W. B. Yeats, 'Fergus and the Druid')

CAESURA   A heavy pause in, or near, the middle of a line.

DICTION   The particular style of vocabulary employed by a poet.

DIDACTIC   Used of a work concerned to expound some moral or political or religious teaching. The term can also describe the tone of a poem if this has a teaching or instructional accent.

ENJAMBEMENT   When the end of a line of verse does not correspond to any natural speech-pause there is said to be *enjambent* (French for 'over-leaping'). A line of which this is true is called a 'run-on' line.

IMAGE and IMAGERY   Terms used in a variety of ways, sometimes more or less as a synonym for 'metaphor' in its wider sense, and sometimes to refer to the creating of 'mental pictures' or to the 'representation of sense experience in poetry'. The words are used with an implied connection with the term 'imagination'.

LYRIC   A name loosely applied to any short poem having some distant resemblance to a song.

METAPHOR   Speaking of one thing, or action, in the terms appropriate to another. Language itself, to a considerable extent, is built up out of metaphor: thus one speaks of the 'head' of a firm or the 'neck' of a jug. In literature a distinction is usually made between a *simile,* in which a comparison or metaphor is introduced by means of the words 'like' or 'as' (e.g., 'the corner of her eye/Twists like a crooked pin') and a metaphor proper, which is introduced without any such preliminary warning (e.g., 'The yellow fog that rubs its back upon the window-panes').

METRE   The commonest metres in English are the *iambic,* the *trochaic,* the *anapaestic* and the *dactylic,* that is to say metres composed of the type of feet known respectively as iambs, trochees, anapaests and dactyls.
Iamb (or *iambus*)   A foot consisting of an unstressed syllable followed by a stressed one. Usually indicated thus: 'Agó'.
Trochee   A foot consisting of a stressed syllable followed by an unstressed one: 'Gáily'.
Anapaest   A foot consisting of two unstressed syllables followed by a stressed one: 'Disinclíned'.
Dactyl   A foot consisting of a stressed syllable followed by two unstressed one: 'Gáily'.
A line of three feet is known as a *trimeter,* of four feet a *tetrameter,* of five feet a *pentameter,* of six feet a *hexameter* or *alexandrine,* and of seven feet a *fourteener.*

MOVEMENT   A useful term for denoting the constantly varying pace of verse. (For instance, one might speak of the 'energetic' movement of a particular line of verse, or its 'impeded' movement, or its 'flowing' movement.) The word is akin to RHYTHM, with the difference that 'rhythm' conveys a stronger suggestion of the regular or metrical aspect of verse.

ONOMATOPOEIA The use (or coining) of words that imitate or echo the sound that they designate. Thus, Tennyson's line 'And murmer of innumerable bees' suggests the buzzing of bees. The term is somewhat unsatisfactory, for it suggests an over-simple approach to the complex matter of the relation of sound to sense in poetry.

PERSONIFICATION Representing an abstract idea in the form of a person (e.g., 'Time', in Yeats's line 'There dreamy Time lets fall his sickle').

QUATRAIN A stanza of four lines, containing rhyme.

REFRAIN A recurring stanza or 'chorus'.

RHYME Rhyme is defined by the Oxford English Dictionary as 'Agreement in the terminal sounds of two or more words or metrical lines such that . . . the last stressed vowel and any sounds following it are the same, while the sound or sounds preceding it are different.' HALF-RHYME is the rhyming of similar consonants but different vowels. For example:

> Little I'd ever teach a son, but hitting,
> Shooting, war, hunting, all the arts of hurting.

RHYTHM See MOVEMENT.

SONNET A fourteen-line poem composed (in English) of rhymed iambic pentameter lines. There are two general kinds of sonnet in English:

1 The 'Italian' sonnet, of which the first eight lines constitute a unit called the Octave and the last six lines a unit, more or less distinct, called the Sestet. The Octave rhymes *abbaabba*, and the Sestet *cdeedc*, or *cdedce* etc.

2 The 'Shakespearian' sonnet, rhyming *ababcdcdefefgg*

SYNTAX Roughly synonymous with 'sentence construction'. The syntax or sentence construction of a poem sometimes draws attention to itself as personal or unusual, and this may mean that it is an important and significant feature of the poem. Thus, in the following lines from Thomas Hardy's 'After a Journey':

> Things were not lastly as firstly well
>   With us twain, you tell?
> But all's closed now, despite Time's derision.

one is struck by the apparent awkwardness and clumsiness of the syntax; and this poses the question whether the awkwardness might not be deliberate and part of Hardy's expressive intentions.

TONE The term derives from the way a speaker uses his 'tone of voice' (cool, enthusiastic, satirical, etc.) to convey his attitude towards the subject of his speech and/or towards his audience. Thus, a poem's *tone* might be ironic, tender, grave, cautious, passionate, etc. It is conveyed to the reader by the various devices of language at a poet's command—rhythm, metaphor, shifts of diction, and so forth.